A BRILLIANT MADNESS

OTHER BOOKS BY ROBERT M. DRAKE

A BRILLIANT MADNESS

ROBERT M. DRAKE

Andrews McMeel Publishing®

a division of Andrews McMeel Universal

Andrews McMeel Publishing
a division of Andrews McMeel Universal
1130 Walnut Street, Kansas City, Missouri 64106

www.andrewsmcmeel.com

16 17 18 19 20 RR2 10 9 8 7 6 5 4 3 2 1

ISBN: 978-1-4494-8480-4

Library of Congress Control Number: 2016946134

Book design: Robert M. Drake

First Edition 2015

Images licensed through Shutterstock, Inc.
All rights reserved to the appropriate copyright holders.
Images appear in no chronological order:
ALISA FRANZ, LEVSKA KSENIIA, JENA_VELOUR, LAVIKA,
NERILU, ABOARD, VIK Y, ZENINA ANASTASIA, VERLEN4418,
ANNA ISMAGILOVA

ARTWORK BY: Robert M. Drake

ATTENTION: SCHOOLS AND BUSINESSES
Andrews McMeel books are available at quantity discounts
with bulk purchase for educational, business, or sales
promotional use. For information, please e-mail the
Andrews McMeel Publishing Special Sales Department:
specialsales@amuniversal.com.

If you have ever had
something inside of you.

Something that does not let you sleep,
something that does not let you
go on with your daily life.

If you have ever had
something inside of you.

Something burning your soul,
something you need to get out
but do not know how.

If you have ever had
something inside of you.

Something. Something. Something.

You just cannot put your finger on it,
then this book is dedicated to you.

The madness is real,
and it is something most people
cannot understand,

but I understand you.

You are not alone.

You never were.

This book
is a representation of daily life.
The repetition of the norm,
the same cycles we go through
daily.

Wake up.
Eat.
Work.
Read.
Run.
Make art.
Drink.
Go to bed.

Repeat. Repeat. Repeat.

This is the madness that devours us all.

I am a product
of what they have made me,
of this routine,
and I am trying
to break through the atoms
to become more.

There is nothing else
but this.

CONTENTS

I want to become
all the memories
that inhabit me:

The forgotten,
the lost,
and the things I thought
belonged to me...
but have far gone away.

All the things
I can no longer write about.

All the things
that take the best of me.

A BRILLIANT MADNESS

You seemed fine
the last time we spoke.

You seemed better,
as if somewhere in this
endless dark space
you found a map,
and it led you
out of this world.

I hope you find what
you're looking for.

I hope you come back soon.

A BRILLIANT MADNESS

ROBERT M. DRAKE

THE THINGS BEHIND HER FACE

Going through hell
is different
for other people.
You have to really get to know
your demons
when you are alone.
Because for them,
hell is a place
you go to when you die
if you are evil,
but to me;
hell is in my head
and she makes it feel
more real
every time
she walks away.

Hell is a series
of watching her come
and go.

Hell is in her eyes
from what she has seen.

And sometimes going through hell
means falling deeply
in love.

THE RAIN RISE

People look like rain.
Falling into love. Falling into pain.
The way you handle
the pain is the art.
The love for anything is the door.
The art of falling without pain
is irrelevant — it will not be.
It never begins or ends the same way.
The art begins the moment
you take your first breath into life.
The art of life is the pain...
Is the love...? Is the cycle...?
It is endless. It is effortless.
The pain is the obvious.
The love is the uncertain.
The antonym. The synonym.
We see it coming, and welcome it.
If it happens the same way each time.
We will not learn, we still,
would welcome it. Life's greatest art.
It will not kill you,
but it will be just enough
to make you want to
break your own bones.
It is powerful enough to
collapse a building.
Powerful enough to end and start lives,
to change lives.
The people look like rain,
always falling into things.
Always dying into things.
Always loving and hurting for things.
Things the rain would fall for,
but would never live to understand.

WHAT REMAINED OF ME

I am convinced
that all of us live
without knowing
who we are,
and it is only
in the end
of something we love
where we seem to find
a little more of ourselves.

You were the hidden
secret
to all the things
I will never know.

You were
what remained of me,
and it is all funny,
too funny
how you are not here,
but I can feel myself
getting closer to you

more than ever,

more than before.

BEYOND WHAT MATTERS

You make me
feel good inside
as if nothing matters—
not the future,
not the past,
and just now,

and right now
it all feels
like I am fatally yours,

like two people
who are meant to meet

and

crash for the very

first time.

BLOOMING ALONE

There are
some things we have
to deal with alone.

Some things
no matter who is involved—

it is

really our own
problem to go
through.

Everyone has to live
this way no matter what.

Ultimately as people,

we have to fill
our emptiness
on our own.

SWEET LITTLE LOVE

It has always
been you
and you have always
been love.

And this love
that violently
screams out of you
is changing me.

It is changing
the way I give
myself to the world.

My sweet little love,
you are the death of me,
but you
have not killed me
just yet.

GENTLE MADNESS

The night
was meant
for people like us,
for people
who use it to get away.

For people
who see themselves
in the city lights
and for those
who lose themselves
in the long walks home.

The night is where
the gentle madness
is
my friend,
and that is where

people

like us belong.

FIND YOURSELF

There are
people who have
been ignored
and kicked around
a few times.

The ones the crowd
will tell you
to stay away from.

Seek those people out,

and find them—

they are the ones

who will change

the world.

LOVE IS A VIOLENT FLOWER

We have a complicated
little thing.

It is a small flame
burning the world,
and it burns the same way
her heart feels when it is alone.

We are meant to be hard
and when I look into her eyes
she makes me feel
as if I know nothing at all.

Love is a violent flower
blooming in the middle
of my bones,

and loving her was something else.
It was some kind of heavy rain
that was meant

to flood out

the impurities in my soul.

DEATH IS TOO EASY

Death is too easy
and too simple.

We all know
how it goes,
but believe me,

the hardest thing
in the world is to live

and to live for something.

Something that burns

the soul,

something hard

to forget.

A WILD DREAM

I could not explain it at all.
No matter what language
or what art.

I could not draw it out.
I gazed at my hands
and thought of how many hearts
I had broken.

I destroyed her,
and then she destroyed me
and there were no words
to be told,
other than she felt me,

I understood her
and we were both sorry
for breaking each other apart.

That I know.

We were

the manifestation of a

wild dream.

OUT OF THE HEART

I look at people,
I look at love,
and I look at lovers.

The way they smile,
the way they cry,
and the way they
fall to rise.

Nothing ever seems
to change.

Eventually everything
looks the same,
until it suddenly
becomes madness.

Until it is out
of your head—

out of your
fucking heart.

FEAR IS THE ILLUSION

There are people
who are secretly
wishing for your downfall.

They are patiently waiting,
thinking,
maybe one day
you will lose it:
your mind and soul.

Beware they are everywhere,
next to you
and in front of you.

There are even some
lurking inside of your heart

and

they call themselves fear.

FLINCHING HEART

I saw her standing
before the gun.
She did not shake.
She did not flinch.
She was robbed of it all,
left alone, numbing.

She pulls the trigger.

Her head explodes
into a thousand birds.

The birds explode
into leaves.

The leaves explode
into stars.

The stars explode
into the dreams
we wake to forget,

and she was the flame

to all beauty

the world chose to ignore.

THE THINGS INSIDE YOU

I am seeking
the same thing
as you.

I do not want to
feel alone.

I do not want to
feel like
I am becoming
a part of the past.

Just never forget me
and I will always
be with you.

I will always
keep company
to all
the lonely things
inside of you.

NOTHING IS SOMETHING

Every day
we hope to do
something different,
to be better.

Though sometimes
we always end up
doing the same thing.

We do nothing
because we feel like we have
nothing,
just impossible dreams.

We have more in us
than we want to believe.

More life,
more fire,
and more soul to burn.

Sometimes nothing is something...

even if we cannot

see it for ourselves.

EVERYONE MATTERS

Everyone has their place
regardless of how we see it.

From the doctor
who saves lives
to the murdering bastard
who kills them.

Everyone is born into love,
it is just
some loves are hard
and cold
and they break laughter
into nothing—
into air.

And some are special
and devour
and curse us straight into
the goodness of the world.

Everyone is born with meaning,
regardless if they burn
everything
into the ground.

Everyone.

KEEP GOING

Sometimes
I wake up feeling
like I need something
to exhaust
the darkness in me.

Because I know
there is a light
somewhere in here,

but it keeps leaving
and it keeps coming back.

And every time it returns—

it reminds me
to keep going,
to keep searching:

for something raw

and

for something real.

IMAGINE THIS OR THAT

Reinvent the world.
Rise.
Destroy it
and then destroy yourself.

Be reborn,
rise again,
and then live a little more.
Feel free.
Learn to fill your heart
and learn to empty
your mind.

Let go and let in.

Disappear and then appear.

Lovers and haters.

Remembering and then forgetting.

And it all sounds like a nightmare,
but this life,
for all that it is,
could not be more beautiful

than that

of what we could ever imagine.

DO NOT SURVIVE

I want to pull you into me.
The way a kiss
pulls the soul out of you.

I want it all,
everything inside.

I want to open my mouth
and see you drowning
in the bottom of my stomach,
where my laughter dwells.

There is no other way to put it,
I want my smile
to burn through your skull
in the worst way possible.

I want you to remember
what it is like to love.

To fall

and

barely survive

the way down.

GO MAD

They tell us
how to live.

What to learn.

What to love.

What to eat.

What to fight for,

and what to think.

They tell us all
these things,
and then they wonder
why some of us lose it

and why some of us

go mad.

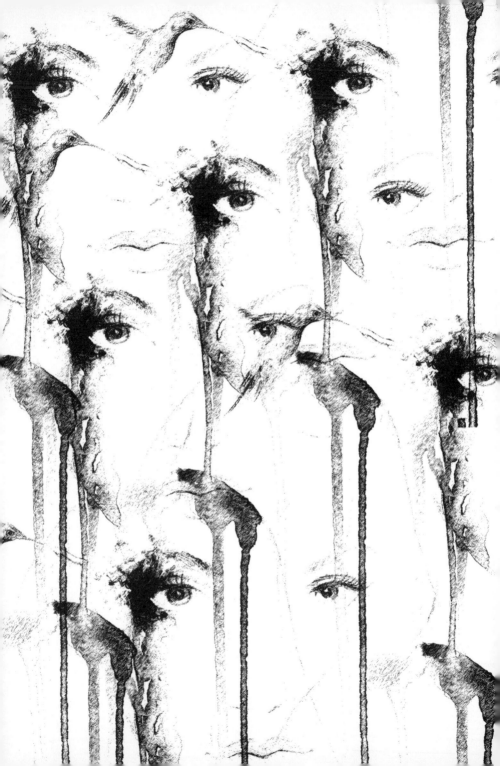

NEEDS TO BE LOVED

She wanted
the bones in my body.

She wanted
my soul
and my mind.

And I gave it to her,
all of me,
all at once.

I did not care,
she deserved it,
and she deserved more.

Sometimes
a strong woman
just needs
to be loved.

THERE IS NOTHING ELSE

And every time
she spoke
flowers would fall
from her mouth.

That is how I knew
I was in trouble.

That is how I knew
I was in love.

Any sweet woman
could terrorize a man,
but when you meet her,
she will dive
into your bones
and kill you
slowly
with nothing else

but words.

I NEED MORE

When I was with people
I would doze off
and look at the sky,

and when I was alone
looking at the sky
I would think about people.

I was never in both places
at one time.

Maybe I was crazy
or maybe I was like
everyone else.

I was not happy
in my own reality.

I wanted more.

DO NOT LOSE ANYTHING

You never completely
feel someone
until you lose them.

And then your tired eyes
become like fire,
and it takes a lifetime
to forget the way they
lit your room.

Hold on to those
who feed your flame
until there is nothing
left but bones.

Hold on to their night
and to their day.

Do not lose them.

Do not lose yourself.

TERRIBLE PLACES

This place is filled
with lost
and twisted people.

They burn from
the inside for nothing.

Fueled by nothing.

Moved by nothing.

I look into their eyes
and see nothing,
but the fear that clings.

I now understand
why people go mad
over nothing.

Sometimes the mind

is a terrible place.

MAKE ME FEEL SOMETHING

Remember this
and remember well.

It is, after all,
a lonely world.

A world where two people
can share the same heart,
but there will always
be something missing.

The saddest of the sad
is how eventually,
we as humans
outgrow the things we love,

and all we could do
is remember

how they once made us feel.

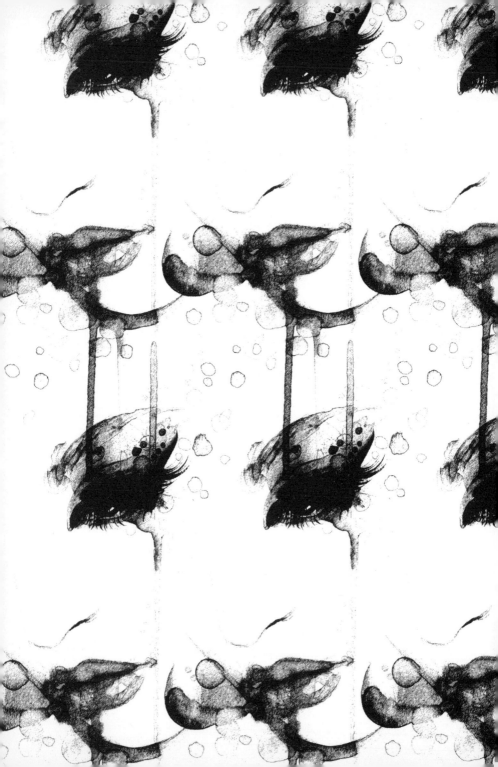

WAITING GAME

She has been
waiting for you
just as long
as you
have been looking for her.

Find her.

Die for her.

Keep her.

Life will be better
when she is around,

what is left of it

can still become interesting,

can still

become more.

SPACES LEFT ALONE

There is a space
inside of us,
one that no matter
how close we get to
other people,

this space can only
be filled
by our own laughter
and our own sorrow.

It is something
we cannot depend on other people
for.

It is something

we have to

make sense of by ourselves.

NO FACES

I see these people
everywhere.

They have hollow faces
and hollow hearts.

Some even have hollow bodies,
there is no soul.
No goodness,
just confusion and questions
and answers
that break into the air.

I see these people
everywhere.

I see them all in me

and

I see them all in you.

FLOWERS ON THE SKULL

She was made
of all complicated things,
but she always
had a simplicity
in the way she laughed.

And that is all she ever wanted,
for someone
to understand her
while she was out
making sense of her soul

and the handful of flowers

blooming

from the top of her skull.

MORE YOU PLEASE

I have heard so many people
say the same thing,
do the same thing,
over and over
that I was beginning to do
and say the same things myself.

People will do that to you.
Most become what they hear
and see.

You have to really
know yourself not to follow
the crowd,
and you have to really
know the crowd to find yourself.

The world is filled
with these kinds of people.

The world needs more of you

and less of them.

FIND SOMETHING REAL

People are no good
when you are doing well.
They want to bring you down.
They want your blood.
They want your bones.
They want to consume you
for your all, for your art.

I get you when you say
you like to be alone.
Most offer nothing,
too much of what people like us
don't need.

Too much emptiness
in their hearts
and in their souls and minds.

Things that don't interest the fire.

People like us should be rewarded.

We see through the bullshit
and always find
something real.

BIRDS ON THE GROUND

We have had
better days,
but one day
I will understand you,
and I will laugh with you
and we will open our hearts
and see each other
for the first time.

Until then,
I will remember you
for the birds you left in my skull,
and for all the times
I let your photograph
slip through my fingers.

I will remember you.

I will remember not to forget.

HOW IT STILL IS

I got older.
I realized how bad it was.
I lost a lot of people
growing up.
Some would smile
and then try to destroy me,
destroy themselves.

I had to learn
how to tell the difference
between laughter and screams.

Between a flower and a knife.

Between a violent welcome
and a gentle good-bye.

That is how it was.

That is how it still is.

FLAMES STAY INSIDE

What most fail to understand
is how to handle
all that fire in them.
All that passion, rage, and love.
They want to let it all out
at once
without knowing about the flame.
Most burn for something,
while others burn for nothing,
and they will both continue
to burn in the grave.

Life is strange,
all this light inside
and we still don't know
what to do with it.

We still don't understand it

at all.

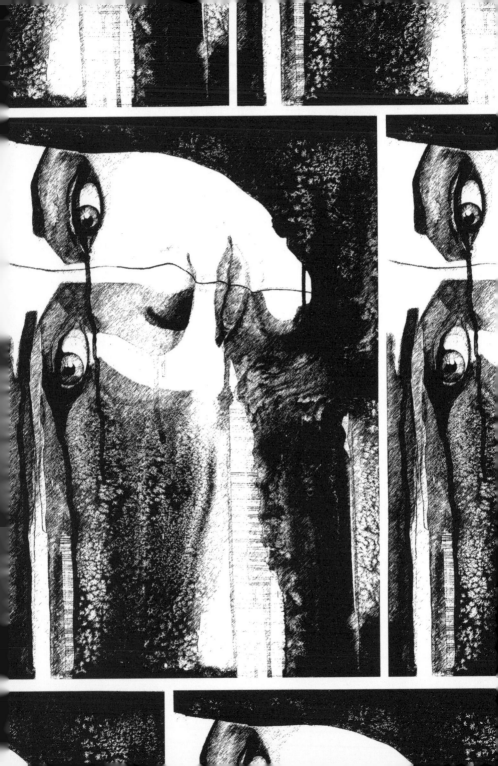

EMPTY WORLD

No one gets it.
No one understands
the way I see it.

I look into the world,
the art is gone,
the religion is gone
and the peace
and the goodness.

It is all gone.

All that remains are faces,
they are blank
and they want to burn for glory,
for something more.

The soul is lost

if the heart is lost.

The soul of the world

is gone.

TWO FACES TWO HEARTS

Beware of those
with two faces.
For they carry two brains,
two hearts, and two souls.
They carry a different
kind of chaos.
The kind that devours all things.
They do not understand.
And then,
there are those with no soul.
Beware of those as well.
For they carry no brain,
no heart and they just follow
the crowd in search for a face.

Do not trust those people
or anything without a soul,
let alone two.

Never trust their destruction,
their hunger to cause horror
will never be complete.

RAIN FALLS

The rain
will always
share a better story,
believe me,
this I know,
but tonight the sky
has no sorrow to tell.

Tonight
is all about
the ones who worry.

The ones who worry
about losing
the people they love.

SANITY IS A BLESSING

To the unborn.
Our madness
will become yours.

It is all the same
and it always will be.

The same love,
hatred,
war and peace.

The same bodies,
faces,
eyes and smiles.

Since the beginning of it all.
Life will always be
an endless cycle driven
by the same ambition
and dreams.

And it is a shame
how we know this,
and still,
we have no idea
how to become
something else.

HOLD WITHIN

The blood will carry
some bad memories,
this I tell you,
and every now and then
you will bleed out
and everything
will flow out of you again.

It will hurt
and like all things that hurt
they cannot be forgotten.

They wait behind our faces,
our eyes,
and in our veins.

Some things,
even in death cannot be ignored.

It is that simple.

It is that perfect.

Everything that hurts
is usually everything

we hold within.

SECOND CHANCES

If someone
lies to you,
fucks you over,
and takes everything
from you.

Do not
give them a second chance.

Second chances

are for assholes.

DISTRACTIONS

I wasn't all there
and she wasn't all there
either,
but we both pretended
to be.

And in a strange way
that was good enough
for me.

People are like that.
They become attached
to anything at any time.

Music.
Art.
Love.
Money.
Sex.

Whatever it is,
people always need something.
Something to distract them
from the truth,
from what hurts.

Something to distract them
from being themselves.

JUST LOVE

Two souls, hers and mine.
Two friends becoming more,
becoming lovers,
becoming more than
just two people waiting to die.

Doomed to our graves
since the beginning.

This mad circus.
I chase her
and then she chases me:
there is no end.

We were two people
sharing one dream.
Two flowers being pulled
from the burning earth.

Two flowers like no other.
Two flowers bleeding
from the roots whenever it hurts,
and it always hurts.
This life means nothing
and we will risk it all

for a chance to love.

NOT ALONE, NEVER

Nothing is as terrible
as thinking you don't deserve

the love you have been given,
or the people,
or the things that make you who you are.

If you have it,
it's because that's the way
it was meant to go.

Any other way
could possibly cause some kind of awful
disaster somewhere
around the world.

You have to let things
happen on their own,

even if you think

they do not belong to you

at all.

I FEEL YOU FEEL ME

You think
the world doesn't
get you,
but it does.
People do
the same things.

They worry about money.
They worry about love.
They worry about their future,
their jobs,
and not being alone.
They worry about
where they are going tonight,
who they are meeting,
and why.

People feel the same way.

We all do.

You are not alone,

you never were.

WOMEN

To the women.

They all look like flowers.
They all look like miracles.
They all look like laughter.

Like the rain.
Like the fire.

The sisters.
The mothers.

On this day
and on all days like these,
the women,

they all look like
the things our hearts are
made of.

Cherish them daily,
and if possible,
dearly.

They are the image
of whatever goodness
there is left

in the world.

LOVE YOURSELF FIRST

I think
you are looking for something,
but you do not know
what it is.

I think maybe
that is why you cling
to certain kinds of people,
to secure something in yourself
that you are doubting.

Perhaps,
in some sense,
you doubt your own future
which is why
you always find yourself
in the hardest situations.

And then,
you wonder why they leave.
You wonder why they do not need you
or love you.

The truth falls heavy.
It is not that they do not love you,
maybe you,
my dear,
still have not learned
to love yourself.

ONLY ONE LIFE TO LIVE

For the sake of your own life.
If you have something to say,
then say it!
Life is too short
to make it flow silently
in darkness.
Believe in your voice,
the one blooming inside
your skull.

Do not let their cruelty
damage it beyond repair.

What dies will die,
and what does not
will eventually,
but what you say
will go on forever.
It will violently echo
like laughter,
like the kindness small things bring.

Your words,
let them go
and soon enough,
their meaning will find a way back
to the light.

Fight for the things that live inside you.

That is the only thing left to do.

NEVER GIVE UP

If they can run with you
then that is how
you know you have found
a soul mate,
a person with the same story.

And they are not lovers,
soul mates are never lovers,
but people who understand
the struggle,
your struggle.

They come from the same edge,
they are built from the same fire
and walk through
the same line
looking for others like them.

Sometimes they come
into our lives for a moment,

sometimes a moment can last a lifetime.
This we must understand.
Soul mates are people who remind us
how we are not meant to die alone.

They are the only reason
why we should never give up.

GOOD TO EACH OTHER

I felt a sting,
it came to me
the same way she came to me,
like some kind of terrible accident.

I could not sleep.
Days like nights
and nights like days.
I knew from that moment on
I was in trouble, incomplete.

I had experienced a small amount
of pain
when she would leave,
but no one ever stayed,
and if they did,
eventually,
I would want them to leave.

The things I wanted
could never adjust to the things I needed.

She was only good to me when
I felt alone,
and I was only good to her
when she needed a lover.

We were only good to each other together.

Everything else was shot to hell.

BURN TO THE GROUND

Every hour.
Every minute.
Every second.

We are transforming
into other people.

So maybe the next time
we meet
I will be someone else.

I will be better.
I will be different.

Maybe next time

I will be a spark
and I will burn this
fucking

world to the ground.

THE ONES WHO LOVED

We were the ones
walking through hell,
walking out of it distorted,
broken
and with our heads on fire.

The ones who died
a little each day
and had to learn how to deal with it.

The deranged.
The confused.
The lost and the forgotten.

We were the ones
they would call mad.
We were the fallen,
the ones who did not sleep,
and still,
would dream.

The ones no one understood.

We were sinking into each other,
and no one knew how to save us.

We were the ones
who learned
how to love.

BECOME SUN

Nothing is real.
This life is not real,
but the love you have inside you,

that is real,

and it is a beautiful thing.

Filled with kindness.
Filled with goodness.
Filled with all the laughter
and all the strength
I need.

It gives me the courage

to get up

and

rise again.

NOTHING LIVES HERE

Nothing matters.
Not the things you leave behind
or the things you take with you
in death.

Not their terror
or the things they want you to see.
Not the way the lonely live,
quiet and sad.
Not the things that make us angry
or the things that make us happy.

Not the art
or the way it flows.
Not the slow hours
or those last seconds that kill.

Nothing matters.
Nothing lasts.
Nothing made out of nothing,

but one thing is important,
one thing does matter.

The way you see yourself.
The way you believe.
The way you make others believe.

All else changes.

All else goes on.

FALL TO BEGIN

Sometimes
I think about the people
I used to be
and sometimes

I think about
how many of them
I had to end.

And I often think about

how many more
I must become,

until

I finally learn how to let go

and begin.

WHAT IS FREE

All the sadness
in the world is bearable.
The pain and the regret
are the things we fall into.
The happiness and the wholeness,
this, too,
we fall into.
We are broken.
We are lonely,
but all the sadness in the world
is bearable.

I feel like you and you feel like me.
We feel like the rain.
We are always falling.

In and out of things.
In and out of people.
In and out of ourselves.

We wait for these things to happen.

There is a profound genius
in the way we wait.
The way we endure, it is an art.
The pain is an art.
The love is an art.
We die and then, they are both gone,
but still we carry the sadness,
and still, it is bearable.

It is what makes us who we are.
Accepting it will always be
the ultimate form of freedom.

2002

I have this letter you wrote me.
It is from 2002.
I take a look at it sometimes
and it reads how much
you wanted us to work.
Well, things did not work,
and it is funny how several years later,
things still do not work.
At least not the way I expect them to.
I laugh,
not because it hurts,
but because of the fact that we lost
whatever it was
we wanted back then.

Dreams become long whispers
and lovers become distant places,
lost places, forgotten places,
and ones never to be called home again.

It is nothing new,
memories devour,
and they can kill.

I had you, I was very close.
Now all I have is this letter.
There is nothing else to say.

I am sorry for all the misunderstanding

I might have caused.

WHEN WE WERE YOUNG

People look at you different,
like you are someone
they used to know.

Like you went away
and came back strange
and odd.

And they don't like it.
They say they miss the old you.
They miss the way
you used to smile
and laugh.

And it is funny
how you think
and say the same about them.

You miss the old days.
We all do.

We miss the way
life used to make us feel

when we were young.

I WANT TO LOVE YOU

I know you are living
with something
inside of you.
It is not what you think it is.
You want to think you are lonely,
but you are not.
You feel like that is the only way
you could describe it:
being broken and empty,
but that is not it.
You are afraid of it
because you know it could destroy you.
And I am afraid of it too,
that is why I do not let it out.
I keep it caged where no one will see it.

You are a lot like me.
You are afraid of being understood.
You are afraid of someone really being there
for you.
You are afraid of the love inside of you,
accepting it, becoming it.

You are afraid
but I want to try.

I want to love you.

Anything else
would not make
much sense to me at all.

BECOMING MORE

You will always be
changing, transforming,
and shifting:
here and now and later.

Forms will always be mixing,
colliding,
exploding into the air.
Crashing into the waves,
in and out of the madness.

In and out of
the maddening wait.

The wait to bloom
and grow and stem out
of the burning earth.

It is a beautiful thing.
A miraculous thing.

Find it...

and maybe tomorrow
you will be someone else.

That alone is everything worth waiting for.

The hurry and the wait
to become more
than that
of what you are.

TO BE IN YOUR LIFE

There are so many
lonely people.
So many lives out there,
looking for something
to share.

I remember
when I was a part of your life,
and now I sit here
looking at your photos:
the old and the forgotten.

You have grown
and I, too, have grown.

I wonder how things
would be
if I had met you a little later
in life.

Maybe you wouldn't be
such a distant memory,
and maybe I wouldn't feel
like I could have done

a little more

to make you stay.

LEAVE BEHIND

Love was one of those things.
It was always moving inside of me.

Wild and strange.
Weak and strong.

Yes, I felt it before.
I wasn't all that hard.
It was there, alive and well,
pushing to come out.
Pushing for ways
to find itself back into my life,
but I didn't let it in.
Things weren't that simple.
And she couldn't imagine
how hard it was for me to love.
I just didn't know how to control it,
she didn't know how to control it,
but most people do not know
how to control it.

Love was one of those things.
The moment you had it,
you lost it.
And most people were afraid
to become
the things it would leave behind.

SO MUCH TROUBLE

This hell.
This fire.

Inside and out.

Lovers betray you.
Friends betray you.

And sometimes
you even betray yourself.
You have to really trust yourself,
but how could you trust yourself
when you get yourself into so much trouble?

Lovers love you. Lovers hate you.
You want them and then,
they become useless to you.
You want the world
and the world wants you.
The same way you want a lover
to lay with you at night.
People betray people,
but you should not betray yourself.

Trust yourself. Trust that feeling.

Inside and out.

It may be
the only reason why you
are still alive.

LOVE AGAIN

Listen kid.

You have to do things
for yourself before you
do things for other people.

Love yourself,
then love other people.

Trust yourself,
then trust other people.

Be kind to yourself.
Be good to yourself.

When it is time for other people,

it will be time for other people

but right now you have to save
yourself before you can save

other people.

MEANT TO END

There are too many
misleading things in this world.
Too many
useless moments,
and too many moments
that are not lived
too well.

If you are going to live
for something,
anything,
at least let it go
beyond the brain.
Let it begin and let it die
beyond the body.

And in the end,
you will end,
where you are meant to end.

There is nothing
more beautiful

than that.

CONNECTS TO EVERYTHING ELSE

When it hurts
they will feel you
and when they finally understand you,
for your all,
they will accept you.

People are like that.
The moment they know your story
things ease up a little.
They have compassion,
it is built in them
and it is something no one could ever
take away.

Everyone has this power
and it is strong enough to change the world,
to save the world,
in all its burning madness.

This can possibly cure
all human suffering.

Compassion.

It is one of those things.

It is the bridge that connects
everyone to everyone else.

BELIEVE IT IS YOURS

I understand you.

Solitude can be
a bitch sometimes.

It can give you
all the beauty in the world,

and take it all
away
the moment you
believe it is yours.

LIVE AT ALL

You keep searching
through your brain
for all the answers,
and it feels like walking
through a desert:
alone and empty.

You have forgotten
about your heart.
The same way you
have forgotten how to live,
but you keep searching.

You search so much
that you barely notice
how far you have come.

People always need
some kind of validation,
and that is the great metaphor
of life:

we live so hard

that we barely live at all.

LIFE ON THE OTHER SIDE

Lost dreams,
lost hearts,
and lost minds.

Everyone is living
inside of something
or someone.
Walking slowly,
searching the searched.

Over and over,
and all we could do is wait.

We wait
till one of us escapes.

We wait
till one of us returns

and

we wait
for something
or someone to remind us
what life is like

on the other side.

CONSUMES US ALL

There are times
when we quietly look at each other.
We collect glances
like old souvenirs,
and somehow,
the way we pass by makes us
both feel
so goddamn stupid.

We used to wait hours
to see each other,
and now we look the other way
and pretend we don't exist.

And we don't exist,
at least not now
or maybe not ever.

And I am sure of this feeling.

I do hate you,
but I also love you
and I don't know which one
I want to lean towards to.

I just hope one day
I could see your face without this fire
trapped inside of me wanting to explode.

I wouldn't wish this feeling upon anyone:
dead or alive.

It is the madness that consumes us all.

SUICIDAL STARS

You fill me
and maybe that is why
I feel empty at times.

So stupid and awkward.

I could barely make myself
feel at home
with all the people
and places I love.

I cannot get away.

You are the sky,
the suicidal stars
that never stop falling.

The thought of you
is haunting
and it keeps following

me

everywhere I go.

FULL BLOOM

She is going to find herself
when she is meant to find herself.
In the wrong or in the right place.

In this space or in the next.
Today or tomorrow.

Tomorrow is drowning drunk in love,
in inspiration.
In the things she cannot understand,
but there will always be something
happening to her,
and something will always be changing her.

Something to bring her closer to herself.

She will continue,
she will endure and grow.

And the way she will see the world
will be nothing more,
but a reflection of herself.

And all at once,
the search will be beautiful.

The birth of a flower is one to remember,

the moment
we all
pay attention to her bloom.

SO TRUE

You are supposed to think you can't fail.
That is what they want you to think.
They want you
to believe in all that is pretty
and ignore the ugly.
To believe only in the day
and not the night.
Where they can see you.
Where they can figure you out,
and place you in a room.
That is the way of life.
Their way of life.
We think, we are in control.
We think, we are free.
We think, we know.
We think, but don't at all.
Born slaves.
Born to become lawyers,
born to become doctors,
and teachers, and dentists,
and murderers, and thieves,
and good men, and good women, and more.
Born to become ... anything less than we think
we deserve.
We are supposed to believe.
We do not believe.
We cannot believe.
We cannot see.
It is all a lie.
This life.
The way we think.
The way we walk,
smile and laugh.
It is all not so true.

It is all their born truth.
It is...
all just too useless.
Too hopeless.
Too dark, and yet,
they want us to believe.
They want you to believe,
and me to believe.

To believe.

What is it to believe?

What is it to pretend?

FACE THE WORLD

Wars in the east.
Wars in the north.
Wars in the west.
Wars in the south.

War over sees the future,
and we watch it, as it
laughs to our faces,

we smile.

I look over seas and
see how death is being held
over there,
and then I remember,
how death is being
held over here.

The people on the
other side of the globe fear
the same things as we do.

They fear the loss of identity.
The act of being told who they are.
They fear losing their homes,
their brothers, their mothers,
their fathers, and sisters.

Maybe we are not so different.

We care, and we care enough
to kill each other for the things
we believe in, the things
we live to die for.

NO REASONS

Reasons to be pretty.
Reasons to die slow.
Reasons we need
the world to know
we are here.
To be accepted.
To be adored.
People need people
to fill the emptiness of
the soul.
People need other people
to feel the endless push
and the endless pull.
Too much makeup on the soul.
Hide it all.
Hide yourself.
Your face, your eyes, and
your own skin.
Beneath there is more.
A heart and a mind.
We risk it all to feel.
Reasons to feel.
No one wants that,
to die alone.
Thinking that is suicide.
To be pretty is suicide.
To be accepted is death.
Death is not pretty.
What to do with all
this attention, and this,
and this...
adoration, acceptance.
Nothing.

It means nothing.
It is in our heads.
It is in my head.

It is transparent.
It is artificial.

People need people.
People need love.
They need to love themselves
the way they love what they are sold.
People need each other.
People need someone,
anyone
to tell them they are not alone.

GO ON WITH OUR LIVES

I do not know you,
I do not know me,
and somehow we accept this
and go on with our lives.
We spend too much on too little.
We spend more time with
our phones than with the
people we love.

Too much time on useless things,
mindless things,
to the point where we have
nothing to give,
nowhere to go, and not
much to look forward to.

I think we want to understand
each other, we just do not know how to.

I want to love you.
I want to love me,
but
why is all of this too hard?

You do not know me,
you do not know yourself,
and somehow we still,
accept this

and go on with our lives.

NEXT TIME

She just got out of rehab
the night before.

"What was it like?" I asked.

"It was like holding your breath
in a room full of air."

She was in there for almost three weeks.
She kind of lost it a few days before that.
She tried to kill her body
and release her soul into the air.
She said there was too much inside her:
too much pain and too much love.

She took 19 antidepressant pills
from her mother's nightstand
and drank two full bottles of vodka.

She was serious about it. She didn't care.
Her mother found her nearly dead
before they pumped her stomach out
with charcoal.

What is going on with these
kids nowadays?

They want to die over anything.
Maybe I just don't get it
or maybe they just don't understand
life at all.

"Life is easier on the edge.
People like you live on the center.
You want to see everything
and understand how it all works.
Have a few near death experiences,
and it will help you realize how much
life you have let slip through
your fingers," she said.

Maybe she had a point.
I sat there with her as she asked me
to pour her a drink.

I poured her a drink
and a few seconds later she looked
me dead in the eyes and asked me
to pour her another.

"Maybe next time I'll do it
where no one will find me," she said.

"Maybe that's why you're still here,"
I replied.

Some people never change,
the same way some things just don't.

They never will.

That's how things happen.

That's how things are.

FORMATS

The industry format controls
us all.

The banks control the government.

The government controls the laws.

The laws control the people.

The people control the children.

The children control the imagination.

The imagination controls the dreamworld.

The dreamworld controls the arts.

The arts control the mind.

The mind controls the thought.

And we think we have it
all under control,

but we don't.

Humanity you will
never have it under control.

Control has you by the balls.

ALONE AT LAST

I'm in a room
filled with people.
In the center of the crowd
without saying a word.
Then I'm the weird one.
I'm the outcast.
I see them all drinking
and laughing.
Wearing the same outfit.
Men and women
almost alike.
Pretending to be interested
in what the other is saying.
Forget all of that.
I don't owe anyone anything.
Ask me a question
and I will answer it.
I'm polite and gentle,
but you will never find me
talking to someone to kill time.
Not unless I am interested
and very few are interesting.

Many are the same.
With the same look.
The same face.
The same voice.
The same thoughts
and the same goddamn act—
the guy next to me is doing.
And the one behind
that guy too.

There is no interest.
There is no soul and those
things of the crowd
do not interest the soul.
They do not interest
the fire in the eyes,
and in the heart.
I have no interest to begin
with.

So why the hell am
I even here?

People need to start
being themselves.
People need to start giving
less fucks.
People need to be alone.

I'm gone.

I walk out of the room,
and rush toward my car
and then,

I remember
what it is like to feel free.

OVER AND OVER AND OVER

You will miss me.
You will be back.
They always come back.
They need to come back
to feel better about themselves.
To watch me go mad,
in solitude and in violence.
Then they leave thinking
I am crazy, that I have a
problem, a real problem.
So they say.

I tell them to leave, that
I do not need them, that
I do not need anything,
but my art and some food
and water and maybe even shelter.
They leave in fury.
They leave in rage,
ablaze from not understanding
what it is that I am,
but...
they always come back.
And I am not sure who is
crazier.

They come back to
do the same things
over and over again.

And I let them back in
every damn time
over and over again.

REALITY HURTS

"What is all this about?"
She stayed quiet over the phone.
I hated that about talking on the phone.
I hated that about talking.
The way people would get caught off guard.
They would pause and then not say anything.
I could see her blank face. It was all over her silence.
"So what do you want to do?"
"I don't know," she replied.
Women and men we are all the same.
We eventually do whatever we want.
Once we get comfortable enough.
Any situation is like working a job.
The first week you get there on time,
you do your duties without error, you pay attention,
and you arrive all alert. Then a little time passes
and you get tired of doing the same things.
Over and over. Your mind becomes an algorithm.
It becomes a program. You punch in, you punch out
and in between you try to figure out ways
to beat the fucking system.

It's the same way with relationships.
First few months you're as clean as a whistle.
The next few months you're doing as you please.
Fighting, yelling, coming and going. That's enough
to drive us all mad.

"So tell me what do you want?" I yelled over
the phone. I couldn't take it anymore.

"I just want to be with you," she said.

The next day came
and we never spoke again.

And I think I was okay with that.

I couldn't take it anymore.
We couldn't take it anymore.

MIAMI

If you wanted to make it in music,
you went to New York.

If you wanted to make it in the movies,
you went to Los Angeles.

If you wanted to make it in the other arts
(painting, sculpture, etc.), you went to Paris.

If you wanted to face death,
you went to Miami:
The mad city, ongoing,
flowing.

The men. The women. The bars. The food.
The music. The culture. The sky. The lights.
The beaches. And the air.

It is beautiful enough to kill you,
right there, in the same spot you arrived.

It is one of these things you can't explain.
You have to come down and experience it.

Stay for a while,
Miami will remind you
what it is to fall in love.

FALSE GOD

Their faces say something.
The same thing most want.
They don't want to lose.
There's too much to lose,
there always is.

Control. Money is god.
The thing we don't want to lose.
The god we want to keep.
In our pockets.
In our banks.
In their banks with their debt.
It is all ugly. It is not too romantic.
Not too glorious and holy.

The power is menacing.
The power is not real,
it is not food for the starving soul.
The power is strong enough
to kill a hundred kings with one blow.
We worship the control.
We love and need it.
And then we hate it more.
Hate what it does to us.
We hate how it makes us worship it.

We'll still do it anyway.
That's life.
Money is life.
Things printed on paper worth
less than the money.
No sense.
No cents.

No ownership.
No life.

Money is what makes us.
Money is everything
that destroys us.

Money is the god
we should have killed
many years before
it got to us.

THE PROBLEM

People are ticking.
People are waiting.
There is too much
politics in the way we live.
Too much religion.
Too little money.
Too much war.
Too little love.
Too much darkness.
Too little light.
Too much of anything will kill you.
Too little of anything will kill you.

People want more,
but don't understand
what to do with more.

I get you...

There's so much to do
and so little of you.

That's the problem

and

that will always be

the problem.

DEPENDS ON YOU

Different places
and different people.
It is all useless to step
into new things,
thinking it is exactly
what is needed to remake
yourself.
People and places
are the same.

Different locations,
different skins,
but the same bones.

The same flesh,
the same person
and place in the end.

If you need to find yourself.

Find your heart.
Find your soul.
Find something,
anything,
do not forget this.

Your laughter.
Your perfect fire.
Your growth.
Your love.
Your future.

Depends only on you.

ALL MAD

Sometimes you become
so used to the dark,
you forget about the light.

Sometimes you get so far,
you forget what it is like to be
so goddamn near
to someone who understands.

You get so alone.
You get so quiet.
You get so angry.

You forget why to keep going,
and then you remember
why you are not dead.

It becomes an illness.

The way you come and go.
The way you love and hate.
The way your mind fucks
your heart and your heart
fucks your mind.

One day it will all make sense.
One day you will get so
used to the fact, that you
are you and it is okay to be

a little mad,

we all are.

WHAT WORKS WHAT DOES NOT

People are strange,
they sit on couches
with TVs in front of them
to watch other people.

And at night,
they lay on their beds with their
phones on their faces,
looking into other people's lives,
searching for some kind of validation,
acceptance,
something to awaken their
senses.

People are bored.
People are mad,
insane and sick.

Too busy trying to understand
what others are doing.
Now what a shame it is,
how everyone who sleeps
alone does this at night,
it doesn't let them sleep anymore.

And during the day,
they pick up where they left off,
and they forget to leave their mark
in the world

while they're still here.

PEOPLE PEOPLE PEOPLE

It was all bullshit.
I was surrounded by people
who pretended to be happy.
Who pretended to be doing
so well, it made them sick.

Now you see people like this
everywhere.
They are the ones who talk
about their jobs.

Their lives. Their parties.
Their friends. Their children.

The ones who always complain
about everything.

The ones who live miserable
lives, but smile at the crowd
to fit in.

They made me feel
worst about people.

They die before they learn
to live.

I just wanted to get away.

I didn't want to end up
like them.

NIRVANA

You will learn from the solitude,
how the loneliness is beautiful.
You will learn how it is hard to love
and that is why you feel
so goddamn alone sometimes.

You feel so tired.
You feel so broken and empty.

The broken do not get over the fire.
They become it until
there is nothing left,

but even so
there is something.

A small flame is born when
you are alone.

A flame to keep you warm
from the coldness of the world.
You will learn how the
solitude is a miracle.
How the love for yourself is a gift.

You will learn all these things
in the darkness,
and the pain will no longer hurt.

You will find perfect nirvana,
and
you will never feel the
bitterness again.

WALK THE LINE

We feel alone with
the ones we love.
We feel alone with those
we don't love.

Love only works
when it's on our side.

And it's never on our side.

Pain is a trap. Love is a trap.

Neither are meant to
make our lives easier.
Things are not easy.
If it's easy then stay away from it.
People are even harder.
There are two types of people.
Lovers who make love.
Lovers who can't make love.
None know how to stay.
We spend days, hours, minutes,
and seconds trying to make
them stay.

In short breaths and in long
whispers our brains search
for the reasons why most of us
can't find the peace to remain,
why most of us leave,
and why most of us never

find the heart to return.

THE SOUL OF HUMANITY

Somewhere someone
lost their mind,
got killed in a terrible accident,
or even got put away in jail.

Somewhere else,
someone got accepted
to a university,
got a new job,
and had their firstborn.

People are wondering
about the possibilities,
and tragedies.

And yes,
sometimes things do get worse,
but also sometimes things can become better.
You choose what to give the light to.

What to give the soul to.

And once you figure that out,
you will succeed.
You will make others wonder
how you did it,
and in the end, you will

show them how.

That is the beauty of being
human.

AS WE GO

People want to feel
closer to something,

but at the same time they
are trying to get away.

That's the kind of place
we live in.

No one knows where they
are going.

Everyone is finding
themselves

as they go.

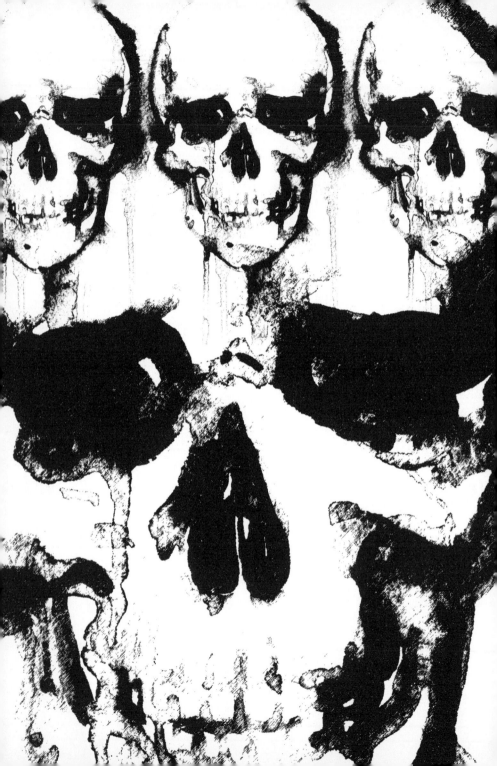

LIFE IN DEATH

It would be good to see you again,
but something inside of me
has not died,
at least not yet.

You didn't take all of me with you.
I am still here,
and something inside of me
is still fighting.

And it keeps telling me
to protect my fucking heart.

So I won't do it.

You don't have a soul.
You're no good for me,
I'm sorry.
And it's moments like these
that matter the most.
Moments when you put
yourself above the mountains
with the gods.
Those moments when you realize
how good you are,
and how some people don't
deserve your goodness.
Save these realizations
for the choices that matter.

They make the difference
between life and death.

LEFT TO GIVE

I am thinking about you
right now and I am sending
you love, real love.

The kind that warms the skin
and waits all night to be held
by the moon.

The kind that reminds you of
how beautiful you are under
the day and the night and
between what is left.

The kind that does not
wake the next day alone.

This is me thinking about you tonight.

This is me sending real love,
all that there is to receive.

The only gift worth sending.

SUNSET IN PEOPLE

Don't let them see you like this.
Don't let them know
how alone you really are.
Don't let them understand you
or know what you feel.
The more people know
the more they could hurt you.
And they will always look
for ways to bury you beneath the earth.
People are like that.
They are cruel and envious.
They want to drink your soul.
They terrorize with love to destroy love.
But not all flow like this.
They're some who
have gone through hell.

They have seen too much,
and they speak about it too little.
They have loved deeply
and know how to divorce real pain.
They are orphans to the crowd.
Let these people in.
Let them drink you.
Dive in and out of you
and welcome them to stay.
They are the ones who will see you without
you even showing them
who you are.

Find them. Love them. Die with them.
Your world will never see
another sunset because of these people.

HARD TO KEEP

She makes me feel
something familiar.

Something untouched.
Something sad and beautiful.
Like seeing an old friend
come back home.

I cannot run away from that.
I want what is easy and simple.

Love is always better
when it is easy and simple.

But when it is hard,
it is precious and delicate.
Unspoken and on the edge.
Life is always better on the edge.
It will make you see what is
worth dying for.

That is all I know.

She makes me feel
alive and dead at the same time.
Blessed and cursed.
Between night and day.
She makes me feel something,
but still, it is not enough
for me to fall in love.

I know how hard it is to let go.

BECOME THE AIR

You tried to change.
I can give you that,
but people don't become
different people overnight.
That's not how it works.
It takes longer days
and even longer hours
to become, but you will
always be changing,
transforming and shifting,
here and now and later.
So it's okay if you don't
like yourself today,
because you will always bloom
out of the dirt.
And wake up daily to a different you.
It will never end.
You will continue to bloom
even in the grave
and flowers will grow
and whisper your name.
In time you will change,
the pain of not knowing
will become air.
And you will become earth.
So keep this in your skull:

maybe today you are you,
but maybe tomorrow you will
be someone else.

That alone is everything worth
looking forward to.

HAPPINESS IS BEAUTIFUL

Don't take happiness
for granted.

Don't let a good day die off
in the burning sunset.

Don't let it fade out of the light
without you remembering
what it was like in the darkness.

Know it.

Know how it makes you feel.
Know it while it's with you.
It's not meant to be yours forever
and neither is the pain it leaves
behind when it's gone.

Know your happiness.
Know your laughter.
Know your own smile.
Know them and
know how to make them stay.

The more they stay
the easier it will be
to watch them come

and

to watch them

go.

DIE TOO YOUNG

We either die
too young
or too old,

and it is usually
caused by two things:

a great lover,

something that made us
feel real

or both.

WHAT REMAINS

Between the hours,
the minutes,
and the seconds.

We are more than
all the places we used to live in.
More than all the people
we have fallen into.
More than old photographs
and more than the music we love.

We are the soft rain.
The endless summer days.
Every nights' late night.
And all the laughter
that fits inside our small bodies.

We are far,
and close from each other.

We will become more than
that of what we could imagine.

To believe in the people
and their goodness.

Is to believe
that we are more
than that of what
remains.

THE WOLVES

When I am with others
I become someone else.

These types of things happen
on their own.
I cannot call it that is how it is.

Different people bring out
different sides of me.
Some I have never known,
and some I have outgrown
and forgotten.

I am a thousand versions of me.
A thousand love stories
and a thousand tragedies.
Surviving all at once.
Fighting the good fight
and dying before the sun rises.

It is no wonder why I still
cannot understand who I am.

The wolves inside me
have gone mad.

They have eaten
themselves
before figuring out
what they are.

THE ART THE POETRY

To the ordinary work experience.
To the timing
and the control.

We become machines of labor.

Clock in, clock out.
Hour after hour.
All we have to look forward to
is a check and the weekend.

Day after day.

And they both do not know how to stay.
They are both lovers,
coming and going continuously.
After that, there is not much to live for.

We fall in love, then we raise a family.
More clocking in and out.
It is almost a suicide.

This makes dying sound too easy.

But the art. The poetry.
Now that can save your life.
And the films and the music.
Sometimes that is all we have,
it is all we need.
Art is the savior.
Take it in as often as possible.
It is, possibly, the only
form of beauty left
in humanity.

THE CROWD

Be careful who you idolize.
There are so many fucked up
people in this world.
Don't be like them.
Most are lost and have to keep reminding
the crowd of their victories.
Keep your eyes open. They are the ones
who keep claiming they are real,
but real people don't do that.
That is not strength.
There is no real power in forcing
others to believe in something you're not.
Beware of these people,
and stay away from them.
They are the most fraudulent people out there,
and they will kill you if they have to,
for nothing. Don't be like them.
They advertise women, money, and fame.
Alcohol, drugs, and sex.
They lack religion and love and peace.
Don't be like them. Don't try to.
They destroy art with a sadness powerful enough
to swallow the ocean.
They judge what they don't understand,
and then,
they admire it when the crowd is gone.

Don't be like them, becoming like them
is a suicide, and what hurts
is how most people
become this way without really knowing
what they have just done
to themselves.

ALL BELIEVE IN YOU

You're not alone goddamnit,
you don't listen!

It's almost like
people know they're not
and still,
they choose to believe they are.

People live inside the mind.

The same way love
lives inside the mind.

So no matter where you are,
someone should always be there

to remind you...

how you should never feel
this way again.

Push them out,
they are waiting,

and

they all believe

in you.

MORE LIFE IN YOU

"He barely fits in his coffin.
They must have done something
to make him fit in that box."

That's what I thought the night of my
brother's funeral.

His body was too big.
He was 6'4".
His life was too big.

The love trapped in his body was too big.
His smile was too big,
bigger than that box
he ended up in.

Now his ashes are in an
even smaller box.

I don't understand how he was contained.
He had too much inside him.

Even in death the world
will make people seem
like their lives are smaller
than that of what
they really are.

STILL ALIVE HERE

They are all doing what
they are doing because
that is what they are meant to do.

They wake up in the middle of the night
to sound the same.
Feel the same.
Look the same,
and when they are asleep
they are dreaming the same too.

But you are something different.

Something beyond the daily life.

You wake up in the morning,
before the sun rises
and birth this violent poetry.

Everything you do is too real,
too human,
and you could
care less of the bullshit people bring.

You are your own killer,
but you have not killed yourself
just yet.

TAKE IT ALL IN

I see the pain
piling down the avenue.
Filling the city,
slowly dissolving
through our fingers.
Through the tears that
cling to our faces and eyes.

We are not too lucky.
We are too obvious.
Everything hurts the way it should.

Some of us die with such a pain.
One that consumes all,
that consumes the flesh
and the bone,
the air and the sea.
and it is never too much
or too little, but just enough.

Take it all in ...

the right amount of it can get you going,
it can change everything.

Sometimes the pain is all
that we need.

BLOOD AND CASH

The companies
want to cash in.
The moment they see
something or someone
getting attention,
becoming famous, and
making some kind of noise.

That is when they come for you.

They want your blood.
They want your heart,
but they are not alone in the hunt.
People are the same.
I have had so many people
contact me.
They try to make it seem
like they are helping me.
Now why the hell would someone
want to help me?
Someone they do not know.

These are facts.

People want to build off other people.
They think I can help them.
I could barely help myself.
People and companies are the same.
They come from the same lineage.
They want what other people have.

They see a future.

One that they don't believe in themselves.

AMERICAN DREAM

Tonight America wants war.
A silent ... vicious war.
One that we are not aware of.
Awareness is golden.
The gold is the freedom,
a luxury we cannot afford.
Those who hear the bombs
know ...

but most don't know
or don't know enough.

There are forces in this world.
In this land.
In our cities and small towns.
They want us to stay in line.
They will punish you if you
cross it, and
they will push you to cross it.
And once you cross it you
will never be the same.

Your eyes and ears will change.
Your hair and the air you
breathe will change.

Change is a war.

America is a dream.
A dream bigger than our own lives.
A dream that explodes into gunpowder.
It fills the rifles.
It fills the blood of these men.

The men who hunger for wars.
The men who hunger for oil and power.

The men who make America.

America wants war.
A war that is not meant to end.
A war with no sides.

The world will be covered
in red, white, and blue.
The only colors that represent peace.

Or so they say.

TOO HARD TO STAY

It is important to visit
that place inside you.

That place no other human
is allowed to enter.

There you will find no fear.
You will find the laughing sun
and you will love there
and rise there and fall there
and break there and put
yourself back together there.

Let that be the only thing
you live for
and let it take you back
where you began.

To begin within,

I swear...

that might be the most beautiful thing
in the world.

RADIOS DO NOT STOP

I know you want it to stop.
The news wants it to stop.
The radios want it to stop.
The blogs and the social media
become the exhausted.
The people are tired.
Born with tired legs and tired arms.
Tired bodies that are too heavy
to move.
Eyes that drag and skulls
that are left behind to follow.
They move slowly,
and
they want it to stop.
But the only way it can die
is if we stop giving in to it.
We stop giving in to the brands.
The things we think are good for us.
We stop shoving our wallets
down their throats.
Our money is their fuel.
Our money is why they exist.
They control it all.
Our money gives them the power.
Power is irrelevant if the
current of money stops.

Nothing else has to die if we stop
fueling their greed.
The war will end.
The killing will end.
The animals.
The food.

The medication
will all be pure.

But how much can we take?
Only our money can stop it.

Stop the madness.
The control.
The agenda.

We have the power to end it,
but we are born to believe it is forever.

Forever is beautiful.
Forever is terrible.
Forever is the madness.

This control, the same way the money flows.

But I can't stop it. Can you?

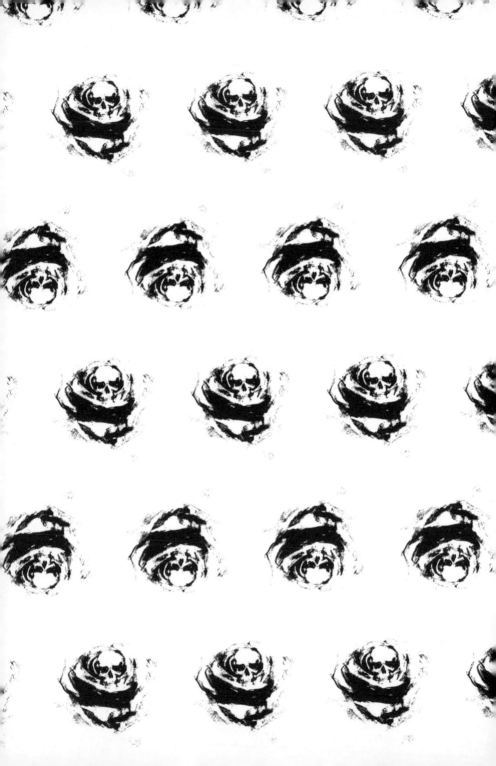

SO MANY DAYS

My brother died,
so now I think about death
almost every day.

I think about it
because it has been a year
since he died
and he has missed so many days.

But if I could talk to him,
I would tell him how
not much has changed
since he died,
but then again
not much ever does.

Life will always be
a cycle of the same things,
and we have all lived
the same life more than once.

In different sections,
and
at different times.

THE MESSAGES

The women are too lovely.
They email me
and always want advice.
Some want to just say hello.
While others ask to meet me.

They don't know anything
about me.
No one does.
I like to keep myself away from
their eyes.
The eyes can play tricks on you.
Don't believe everything you see.

I always reply though.

Sometimes I give advice,
some good, and some bad.
I don't have all the answers.

Then . . .
sometimes I say hello back.
And then they reply back
and I don't reply back.

Can you imagine writing back
to hundreds of messages?

And then, there are the ones
who want to meet me.

Those women must be mad,
willing to meet a complete stranger.

These brave women.
These are the ones the men
should be running from.
They have blood on their faces.
But of course not literally
and
of course I never meet them.

If they are mad enough to meet me
then they are capable of anything.

These strong-willed women.
I would never wish to meet them.
They have enough in them
to ruin a country.
But I wouldn't expect anyone
to understand that.
To understand why I wouldn't
want to meet these beautiful
women.

I am not as lovely as they think
I am.
I am my words:
broken and confused.

Meeting me will just be
another disappointment.

BETWEEN WORLDS

She was trying to find
the connection.
The one between her
and other people.
Between my words
and the heart
that went out of her.
Between the darkness
and the places within it—
to grow in.

And I admired that kind
of passion,
it made me feel good.
The way she knew there was more.
A better love hidden in love.
A better person hidden in a person.

And women often know,
they can feel it in their bones.
There was more to this beating body,
and she understood that.

Ignoring her would have been foolish.

It would have made the graves
appear closer than that
of
where they truly are.

FAMOUS

They say I am famous, that I made it.
I don't feel famous.
I can still walk down the street.
Fame is one of those things.
It doesn't exist. It is not real.
It is in the mind.
Everyone wants to be famous.
But no one understands
how fame brings the worst
kind of people out.

The moment they think
you can help them
they will come for your blood,
for your flesh and skin you alive
for a little recognition and money.
But the moment the fame is gone,
because it is not meant to stay
you become useless again.
You become old
and irrelevant to them.

They are wolves masquerading as humans.

Now we all have heard what
fame can do to a man and a woman.
I just never thought it was real.

And now everyone acts like I owe them something.
I cannot steer the other way.

Fame just makes the bullshit
easier to see but harder
to get away from.

I DO NOT CARE

Now I rest
and I feel heavy,
watching the shoreline
above the sand.

I see the sun setting.
It is falling,
and I, too, am falling.

Falling like the young men
who fight wars.
Falling like the exhausted
and like all things that rise.

I think I am falling,
and it only takes a second
to feel the rush
before it finds its peace in
my memory.

I keep falling.

And there is not a
thing that can stop me

because

I do not care.

COME BACK WITH YOU

But two people
can go through
the same tragedy,
share the same feeling
and understand each other
to the point
where they both become one.

The brave friendship
with another human.

Where they take your horrors,

love them,
and remind you
how you were not born
to walk alone.

They go through
hell and come back with you
no matter what.

TOO HARD TO LIVE

But I am, in all ways,
what I love.

And if that be true,

then I am the late nights:
awake and alone.

I am the books I read:
old and forgotten.

The laughter that remains
in the avenue after dark.
The things that let me be,
they offer peace.

And the art that refuses
to stay in my body,
it always finds its way out.

Those are the things
that consume me.

I am a lot like you,
all of you.

I live for nothing
and everything,

for all the little moments
that are too hard
to live.

THE REAL OF THE REAL

A woman comes to me.

"You write beautifully,
but you write about brokenness
and suffering.

Sorrow and loneliness,
and sometimes,
it is a little too much for me."

All of these human experiences
rolling down the street,
fighting for a chance
to get your attention.

"It all ends in disappointment."

I said.

"Even in writing things are
not as lovely as they seem."

It is all a long thread
of constant suffering.

All else is not real ...

if you do not hurt for it,
then it is not love.

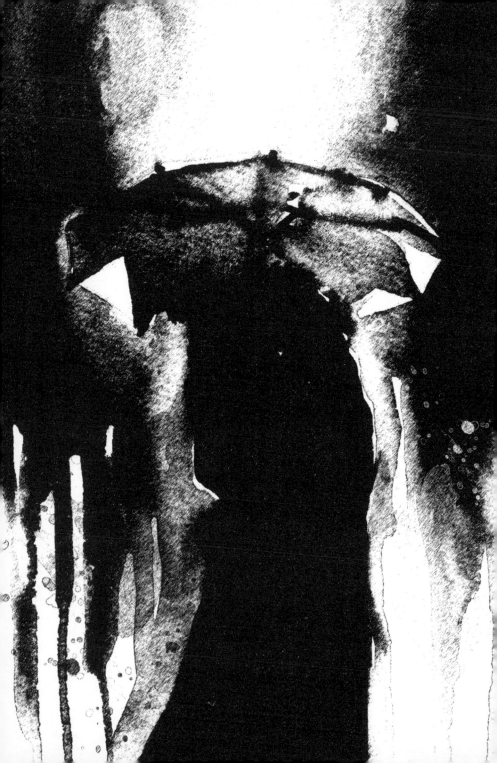

THE EDGE OF THE SUN

We sat on the edge of the sun
like the gods,
and we looked
down upon the earth.

Everything
seemed a little brighter,
the higher we elevated ourselves,

the clearer things got.

We laughed
and we laughed so hard,
because not many know
how much it takes to get away.

Not many know how easy

it is to live, but how hard it is
to understand it all.
The simplest things are
always the most complicated.
And
it could all be so beautiful.

Only if you let it

consume

you.

I CANNOT UNDERSTAND IT

I do have a love for you.

Regardless of how I put it on paper.

I just do not know...

the same way I want
to get away, but
I do not know where to go.

The same way I want
people to listen, but
I do not know what to say.

So when I tell you to leave,
it only means I want you to stay.

But how fucked up am I?
I have to pretend to go mad,
to the point where madness
itself has to pretend to be me.

And all of this, just to try to
make sense of the love I have
for you.

You will never understand it.

Because I could barely
understand it myself.

LOST IN MYSELF

I have nothing left to lose,
nothing left to give
and very little left
to look forward to.
And I swear,
between all those things,
there is very little left in humanity.
My faith in people has dissolved.

There is no lie in that.

And knowing these things,
I rise,
because it is the only thing left to do,
but I am not sure if I care at all.
I just need someone to be there,

fuck everything else.

But still, I choose to ignore
the people who are here,

but there is nothing more
human than that.

There is nothing I can

do

about that.

THE CRITICS

The critics say I can't write
the same way I used to.
That I lost it. That I am not as deep
and profound as I once was.
I have been writing for over 15 years.
I never had it.
I'm still searching for it,
and that is why I still write.
But the experts will say otherwise.
And I cannot argue with them,
they are experts in art
but have never elevated themselves
to make any art.
But yes it is true
because they know it all.
They have degrees in art
but have never experienced
the labor, the sweat, and the blood
that the artist goes through.
But yes, they understand it all.
They bash it all.
They hate it all.
They try to make sense of it,
but they do not understand at all.
It is easier to bury the art
when you do not know what it takes
to create the art.
God delights in us who create.
And I have nearly died four times
because of the art.
The art is the pain and pain is the art
in which we find ourselves.
But what do I know, to them
I am not an artist.

EVERYONE'S FATE

Some good-byes
start something in you,

the kind of thing
you are not
meant to explain,

you just know

you have to solve
on your own.

NO SPEECH IS NEEDED

To the people I have lost,
be glad that you are not here,
for the worst is yet to come.

There will be a time
where we, as people will
not be able to walk down the avenue.
There will be no law.

There will be no freedom:

not of speech, not of religion.

Not of anything that makes us human.
The fear will replace the laughter,
and the violence will replace the fear.
And the people will want more.

Those who have solitude
will dream of crowds.
Those who have fame will
dream of solitude.

In the land and in the room.
During war and during peace.

Global control is a cancer
and it is spreading,

eating the flesh alive.

POETRY STREAM

Tonight, I am here,
and the inspiration keeps
flowing out of me.

The words keep flowing out of me.

The love
and the desire
keep flowing out of me,
and it is constant.

All these things around me
and I sit here
without touching anything,
and yet,
I feel so close to it all.

I feel too much,
I want too much
and the poetry is
the only thing that keeps
me going.

Tonight
it pushes everything closer,
while it pulls
everything further
apart.

THE THING THAT SPOKE TO ME

The vodka
always brought out the best in me.
If I didn't care then I would show it.
There was no filter
between what was right and wrong,
but I knew like everyone else.

The vodka just made everything
easier, and it is sad to say
I needed it to help me get through
the night.

The crowd always pinned me
toward the floor
and the vodka
like the glorious hero it is
always came to save me.

I wouldn't have had it any other way.

Sometimes people need it
to feel better about themselves.
The vodka was continuous,
it was always there when I needed it,
and it always helped me

when I felt most alone,

especially in the

middle of the

crowd.

SHORT AND SIMPLE

Hold on
to whatever
you can
from your past,
because
you're going
somewhere,
and you'll
need something
to guide you
back home.

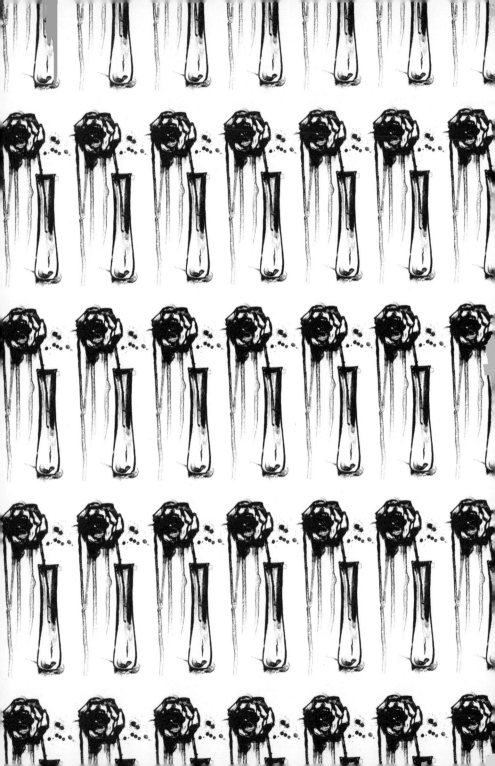

WYNWOOD: WOODTAVERN

I liked being alone,
but sometimes I would
get the urge to go out,
to be where the people
would gather.
The Wood Tavern in Wynwood,
it was always gated with crowds
of people, a wave of bodies
waiting to enter its doors.
The liquor was cheap,
all you needed was 20 dollars
to catch a hell-raising buzz.
Those were always
the best kinds of ways to get off,
the ones that wouldn't
hurt the bank.
The bartender asked what I wanted
to drink. I told her to get me
a vodka and make it a double,
it was going to be a long night.
She came back with a glass
and asked me:
"Aren't you R.M. Drake, the writer?"
I nodded my head.
"Yeah how did you know?"
"You made it, you're a Wynwood
legend."

The crowd caught her comment
and rushed toward me.

I almost fell off my stool.
The solitude is a luxury,
and it is one we barely could afford.

SOMETIMES YOU DO

I met a girl the other night.
She had been reading my work since 2010,
before the social media thing happened.
She had such a knowledge of my work.
She even recited some lines,
lines I had long forgotten about.

"How come you barely write about love
anymore?"

The pause didn't know where to go...

"I just don't feel it anymore, you know...
things change."

"You don't love?"

"Sometimes I don't... Sometimes I do, you know."

For a moment that line could have possibly
saved the world.

Sometimes you do and sometimes... you just don't.

That works with almost everything
life gives us.
The power to walk in
and out of things is a miracle.

The way things change,
and the way we choose
how they affect us once they do.

THE BIRD AND THE SEA

No matter where you go,
no matter where I end up,
I know you will be the same person.
And you will be
made of the same things,
and feel the same things,
and love the same things
as me.

So leave, freely and fastly:

You deserve it.

For I know
you are not meant to be held down.

But what type of monster am I?

To keep a bird in a cage while it dreams
of the sea.

I hope one day you find
where you belong
and I hope you don't regret it.

The sky is waiting
and it keeps calling your name.

NOTHING MORE NOTHING LESS

You think you get it ...

and what hurts most is
that one day you will go through
the same thing with someone else.

You will love the same way.
You will do
and say the same things.

You will chase them
and they will not chase you back.

But right now, you just don't get it,
but one day you will,

that I promise you.

Everything you have caused will find you,

and you will remember this moment
and you will finally understand.

Life is a bitch like that.

Nothing more.

Nothing less.

LOST RAIN INSIDE THE BODY

In the lost hours of us.

I am almost out of the darkness.
I am almost made sick
by the love inside her small body.

It is too much at times.

Now I know there is not much
to say, that has not been said before,
but I swear, she makes living a little easier.
She makes the air
and the pain go down a little easier.

I am sure there must be at least
ten thousand suns inside her body,
and they are beating out of her flesh,
to burn the flesh
and to burn the taste of winter
I have held on to for so long.

If there is any chance of survival,
then I have found it with her.

So the world can go to hell,
I do not care anymore but let her stay.
She puts life where it should be:

in front of all the people who
are searching for rain,
searching for a little more,
and in front of those who keep
searching for themselves.

7 BILLION DESTINATIONS

Against the week
and its days.

7 billion people
walking the earth.

7 billion people
exploding
into the hidden places
of themselves.

Those who know this,
know this well:

how the things that happen
between the brain and the heart
can keep the body up all night...

watching it fade
in all its drunken glory,
to fade back into the light

over and over again.

Wars among wars.

Deaths among deaths.

And not a sound to be heard
as we continue
to transform.

IT CAN BE YOURS

The day is wasted,
and it moves
too fast to figure out
what to do.
By the time you know...
it is gone,
and by the time a new day arrives,
you are moving on
to the next thing.

If it is yours,
then go get it.
Get it while you still can,
while you are sane enough
to remember
why it is so important to begin with.

We have lost too many days
chasing the wrong things.

We have burned the inspiration
on all the wrong things.

Today is the day to make things right.

Today is what we have left.

Today everything can be

yours.

THE MIND IS A TERRIBLE PLACE

A girl once told me she loved me
and that night was the last time I saw her.

If people really understood each other
then maybe loneliness wouldn't be such
a bad thing.

I was thinking of getting a wolf crossbreed
for no reason.

My ex-girlfriend said,
"We would be together forever."
She would say this all the time.
She now celebrates her anniversary with
another man. Seven years later.

Sometimes I stay awake for 48 hours
just to exhaust my body
and sleep for 15 hours nonstop.

If people are running away from something,
run toward whatever they are running away from.

Live dangerously.

THE FAME THE ILLUSION

Some people want
what others have
without knowing what it
took to get it.

Some people want my words.
Some people want my name.
Some people want my mind.
Some people want my fame.
Fame is the measure.
They think it makes everything better,
but they have it all wrong.
Those who have fame
do not want the fame.
The same way those who
search for love will never find it.

Stay away from the things
you want and let the things
you need flow in.

They need you just as much
as you need them.
Time is the bearer.
Waiting is the curse.
Patience is the gift.

Wait for the things you need.

Wait.

Just wait.

It will all soon fall into place.

THE HUNGER THAT NEVER ENDS

The humans want it all.

It doesn't matter if you have enough.
It doesn't matter if your entire
life, you are content with the idea
of having something, something you
don't have or are bound to grasp.

Most people will say:
"That is all I want, and once I have it, then
it will be good enough."

The humans want it all.

They want more money.
They want more power.
They want more affection and love.

More of anything just to say they have more
of anything that means nothing.

The humans want it all.

If they get something they will want more until
whatever it is vanishes into the air.

The humans. The humans. The humans.

Their destruction is one they do not want
but will dive straight into at any moment
and at any given time.

If only it means having more at any moment
and at any given time.

TOO MANY PEOPLE...

I think I feel different now.

Like when it all changes
and it falls on your face,
that moment is priceless.
The moment when you realize
how much you have outgrown it all.

The media is full of shit.
The people are full of shit.
The government is full of shit.
Even the art is sometimes full of shit.

Too many people doing what other people
are doing.

They hardly have a soul,
let alone half a heart.

Too many eyes wandering
and too many mouths running.
They both hit walls
and smash into the dead of night.

But what to do in a place
where everyone wants to bring you down?

You rise and outgrow the things you leave behind.

You rise and let the world burn before your eyes.

You rise and fuck haters hard enough
that their bodies hit where the graves lie.

You rise.

And you will never
stop elevating, not until the sun
claims you
and the gods applaud you...

for almost

kissing the sky.

NAME YOUR GLORY

Maybe you have somewhere you want to go.

Someone you want to share a moment with.

Some dream by some ocean
you want to get closer to

but you feel trapped in a small room,
looking out broken windows for more.

Your entire frame belongs out there.

So keep your mind open
and let the waves of life
gently exhaust your body

and flow.

Flow to get away.

Flow here and then there
but by any means do not let anything stop you.

You have gone too far but not close enough.

Keep fighting...

that is how you will find your glory.

That is how you will hear everything

you want call out your name.

THE FABRIC OF THE ROTTEN

My dog doesn't go to bed unless
I go to bed, poor thing.

I went to a bar and ordered a dirty martini
that was the last time I drank a dirty martini.

Sometimes I want to die
because I feel like I'm not really here.

I saw two people holding hands
walk into a movie theater together,
I thought that was nice.

My mother cannot read English
and she says my work is great.

If someone says they like you
maybe they really do like you.

Inspiration comes and goes,

and...

I'm still

waiting for mine to return.

IN THE 90s

Comic cards were golden.

Wu-Tang really was forever, still is.

Big L died too soon.

The Fresh Prince of Bel-Air was really
ahead of its time.

The summer was the only time
we were able to jump in lakes.

I liked the girl that lived on the second floor.
Everyone used to make fun of her.
No one knew I liked her.

I lost my glasses in the 9th grade.
That fall my lens prescription nearly tripled.

We would stay up late to watch *Mad TV*.
SNL was for old people.

I was Mario Kart champ. Still am.

Roller hockey was our thing.

When we would do graffiti the cops would catch
us and beat us—that was better than getting in
trouble with our parents.

We hated Frank and I think we still do.

ANTICIPATION OF ALL

I think most people are like that.

They worry about things
that might not even happen.

They worry about the future
the same way they worry about
losing something they don't even have.

They become obsessed,
consumed by nothing.

Eaten alive by the worry
and the anticipation.

The anticipation of anything
burdens the skull,
it drags the body across
the burning street.

And letting you in only means
letting everything that fills
walk through the door.

The anticipation

is what kills

us all.

THE BIRTH OF THE NET

If you don't know what A/S/L means
then I don't fuck with you.

AOL chat rooms were always there.
I made so many friends,
some I still talk to, till this day.

CNET was god.

DSL was god.

Napster, LimeWire,
and Morpheus got me through high school.

I wonder how many people pirated Photoshop.

Thank you, Sean Parker,
you belong in Mount Olympus.
I see you getting drunk
and high with Zeus all year long.

I still don't understand PC gaming,
but I know it rules console.

Checking someone's AOL profile to see
if the relationship status has changed.

The dial-up noise
and logging on to hear the loud
"you've got mail" audio—
that made the internet better.

When you had a buddy list

and it was 300+ people.
There was always someone online to talk to.

My screen name was intensechemicalz.
I cannot remember why.

Xxhosplayboychik I still have love for you.

AOL 9.0 optimized was the last update.

It was so hard to say good-bye.

2 MINUTES OF PAIN

Come here,

I want to talk for a while
without watching you go.

Stay with me

and I will show you how
some stories do not need to end.

How some stories do not need
hundreds of pages to be told.

How a thousand lovers could taste
the sky without leaving the ground.

I drink to your love tonight
and all the lovers across the globe:

dead and alive.

Tonight they are all so beautiful.

It is this thirst for human connection

that drives us all.

HIDDEN PROMISE

"I hope things never change between us."

She said as we stayed in bed,
looking at the ceiling covered in sheets.

The room was cold and dark.

"Everything changes, and
hoping they don't, well,
that's the kind of thing that kills people,
and I hope you never die.
So live on and burn well,
because if we never see
each other I want to remember
you for the way you made me laugh
and the way you made me believe
in something again."

That alone made change
something easy to go through.
I did not fear losing anything,
if it went, then it was its time to go.

That's life
and sometimes that's love.

THOSE BAD DAYS

Everything costs something.

Being born was an exchange
for death.
And death was an exchange
for immortality.

That is, if you played your cards right.

And then, I lived,
and time brought age
and age brought experience.

And experience brought pain
and pain made me appreciate love
and love made me afraid
to lose everything.

Everything was always bringing
something.

And if something did not bring
anything: no growth or experience,
then it only brought the graves closer.

Every day death is closer.

And

I see death and sometimes
it looks more promising
than this small room I was born
to call home.

IT IS ALL LOVE

It is a shame how nothing lasts.

Everything good ends too soon
or does not begin at all.

It is hard to welcome anything
knowing this.

The world will end in flames
and so will we.

Our bones will be devoured
by love and the pain will bloom
like a garden full of roses.

We risk it all for people.

We risk it all for one to hold,
and still, we leap off the edge
to taste the sun.

The world will end in flames
and so will we.

Our days are dissolving ...

now let us disappear
from here.

WOMEN I DO NOT KNOW

To the woman I thought I loved:

Do not think for one second I miss you.

Do not think for one second
I am writing about you.

Do not think you are the cause
of my life's work.

Do not think it hurt me,
because it didn't.

Do not think I mentioned you to previous lovers.

Do not think you live somewhere in my heart.
I killed you a long time ago.

Do not think you are different,
you are all the same.

Do not think.

Do not think.

Do not think.

That will make the world a better place.

IT IS NIGHTTIME

You cannot fight racism with racism.
That makes no sense at all.

The 90s was the last great decade.
I don't see any other surpassing it.

I don't see kids playing outside anymore.
Childhood is a rare thing.

Illmatic is possibly the greatest album of all time.

In 3rd grade I stole from my teacher.
I took an extra chocolate bar,
the fundraising ones.

Sometimes I see things I shouldn't:
paranormal things.

When I speak I lose track
and forget what I was talking about to begin with.

I don't care if people don't like me.
I like me, enough said.

When I was young my cousin
and I would get into a fight weekly.
Kids nowadays can't defend themselves.

I feel like I'm not from this planet.

Sometimes I stare at things
and ignore the world.

TO BE CONTINUED

Love betrays.
People betray.
Jobs betray.
Thoughts betray.
Dogs never betray.
Cars betray.
The human heart
sometimes betrays.
Too much alcohol will betray.
Places betray—
when you outgrow them.
Feelings betray.

Everything betrays
and you will betray
yourself if you think
anything different.

Nothing lasts,

do not trust anything.

Now carry on
and
walk away from here.

REMEMBER GROWING UP?

Remember the first day of school?

Remember how bad it was to know you had
a week left before summer vacation was over?

Remember how summer used to feel as a kid?
And how thunderstorms would
sweep the night. Those were good nights.

Remember staying up late?
And when your friends stayed over at your house—
it was the best thing in the world.

Remember what it felt like when you
first learned to ride a bike?

Remember the first time you went
to the pool at night?

Remember the first time you did
something dangerous?
Like climbing up a roof
and staying up all night with a group of friends.

Remember swimming in a lake?
And how you thought you were going to die,
but you didn't.

Remember your first fight
and how your friends backed you up?

Remember television when it was really television?

Remember music?
When it really meant something special?

Remember the 90s?
It felt like a completely different world back then.

Remember those kid arguments over
baseball games or comics cards, dolls, games, etc.?
They were so important to us back then.
Now we argue about money
and paying bills.
What happened to us?

Remember.

Remember what it was like
to see the world with such
enthusiasm.

Remember what it was like
to be a child.

Remember how important it is
not to lose your inner child?

Remember,

try not to forget.

THE STREET IS EMPTY

I walk across the street
looking for the other pieces of me.

Like some half-devoured human,
limping, dragging my body through
the city, searching the searched,
going to places I have been to before
in hopes there will be something
different this time.

I find nothing. Everything always falls
into this category:

half-empty people, half-empty
bottles, and half-empty opportunities.

Nothing fills anymore.
Nothing makes whole.

It makes me wonder if I am ever meant
to feel as one

and knowing

this I still search and search
for more.

Sometimes hope is the only reason
we wake up,

the only reason why some of us
cross the street.

EARTH LIKE A COMET

The ones who stood still,
were the ones
thinking of what to do next
and the ones who were running
did not
have a place to go
but they just kept going.

The same way some people live their lives
without knowing what will happen next.

No rules, no plans, just movement,
and
living like that was enough to make me happy.

It was enough to make me understand
how some things cannot be thought out,

how some things are meant to happen
and how some things hit your world
like a comet
and change its course forever.

That kind of thinking kept me going,

it kept me alive.

THIS IS NOT YOUR REALITY

Stop thinking it is the world.
No one is out to get you.
No one wakes up and
thinks of ways to bring you down.

Maybe it is you.

The way you attract all this
negative bullshit
is killing you faster
than you think.

And you have the nerve to blame
other people,
and other things you do not
even understand.

You put yourself in certain situations
and you are not
thinking of what is happening around you.

You create the world you want
to see.

You get rid of anything that
does not give it, its meaning.

Your world is better than that.

ONE THING CANNOT GET OLD

People get old.
Cars get old.
Towns get old.
Politics get old.
Love gets old.
Music gets old.
Friends get old.
Eventually everything gets old
but orgasms
those never get old.
They never bore.
People are always
looking forward to having them.
The thought walks
through the brain
and the anticipation
pulls on the bone,
and the skin, and
for a split second,
when it rises we
go in all the way.

We forget everything.

Too bad it only lasts
a few seconds.
If they were longer
men and women
would be different.

The world would possibly
collapse from being too perfect.

HIP-HOP

KRS-One is the teacher.

Slick Rick is the ruler.

Ras Kass is van Gogh.

Tupac was our Malcolm.

B.I.G. was the old king.

Nas is the new king.

Big L was street struck.

Wu-Tang is forever.

A Tribe Called Quest was out of this world.

Jay Z is unreasonably dope—no doubt.

Canibus was the beast from the east,
but LL Cool J still knocked him the fuck out.

Cypress Hill got me high.

Snoop and Dre had their own thing.

I was too young for N.W.A.

Mobb Deep had shook ones running.

I wasn't into Ice T or Ice Cube.

DMX, The Lox, and the Lost Boyz were golden.

Eminem was the last of their kind.

Hip-Hop has changed.

Things always change.

When Hip-Hop changes; everything else changes
and
the people haven't been the same since.

THE ACADEMIA OF 24 HOURS

The Internet is a marvelous place.
You can almost find everything you are looking
for there.

Sometimes I google my name to see what I find.

Facebook used to be for college kids.
Mark, you are a genius.

My dog has an eating disorder.
I have an eating disorder,
I wonder where my dog got it from.

I wrote two novels using my phone.
The times are changing.

YouTube is a godsend when you cannot sleep.

Is organic food really organic? Who knows?

I have dreams with my brother too often.
I like to think it is him entering my consciousness
just to make me laugh.

Getting old sucks.

Watching people you love get old sucks even more.

I hope you have a nice day.

I hope today someone tells
you how important you are.

You are important.

SCROLL ON OVER

Little wild girl with wild hair,
I see what you are doing.
I see what you are looking for,
what you want.

I see you smiling with friends,
smiling with strangers, but no
one really notices you,
and that is the real problem here.

I see you, while no one else does.

You are more.
You are marvelous.
You have the sun inside of you
laughing at the sky.

I can feel it.

You are some kind of wild dream,
trapped in some kind of wild girl.

And tonight is one of those nights.

Maybe we are supposed to meet.

Maybe that will give me peace of mind.

I just can't take my fucking eyes off you.

NO TIME TO BREATHE

No time to live.
No time to sleep.
No time to love yourself,
eat or dream.

People, almost all I know,
live too fastly.

Once given anything that
requires a little time,
they tend to lose their
goddamn minds.
But I, too, am like this.

I cannot wait, waiting pulls out
the rage and the madness
and the chaos
and it is ferocious.

And I think I want you.

I just do not have the
time to fall in love.

TAKE ME NEAR

You could take me
far away,
but I know I will not be
far enough.

Keep me away
from it all,

but only leave a few
good things.

Leave me a good book.
Leave me God.
Leave me shelter,
food, and water.

Take me away from the crowd
and everything else
that exhausts the goodness
in my soul.

You only need a
few good things to survive,

and I know people
is not one of them.

THIS WOMAN

To all who know her,
and to all who have yet
to meet her.
I will tell you
this woman is no sweet flower.
She can take laughter
and make it something else.
Make it something the gods
would go insane over.
She carries beauty
and it is thrown around as if it is useless.
Nobody cares, she thinks,
no one is watching,
but I'm watching:
with my hands and soul,
with my all.
Her smile feeds me.
I need it to survive.
To stay alive.
It is that powerful.
It is that satisfying.
This woman's essence:
it is everything.
It is everything I am not.

I think I feel her.
I can feel her flowing
inside me, inside us all.
How could this happen?
I will tell you ...
this woman is no ordinary woman.
She takes laughter
and makes it something else.

She makes it sound
a lot like love.
Like Sunday morning
after a legendary Saturday night.
She makes love
sound like it is a good
idea. Maybe it is or
maybe it isn't, but
that doesn't matter.
I'll do it anyway.
People do whatever they
feel: good or bad.
They do it. Love makes us
do it. Love is a stupid
little thing.
It makes us do stupid
little things.
We know this
and still, we do it.
We fall in love.

Stay away from her.
This type of woman is trouble.
This type of woman has something.
Something I am missing.
Something that has to
do with everything.
This woman is no good,
they tell me.

This woman I have been
looking for my entire life.

RIDE LIFE LIKE THE WAVE

You have got to
flow into life.

Flow like the wind.
Flow like the ocean.
Flow like the blood inside of you.
Let all the moments rock off the deep end.
Rock back and forth,
till you have fallen with love,
and you have caught yourself in
something endless,
in something unexpected.

Life can feel relentless
and
getting through it might be
impossible,
but riding its waves can be
the greatest joy imaginable.

Ride it with passion.

Ride it with no fear.

Ride it until the sunshine goes away,

till the moon crumbles
and the night sky reminds you
of the day.

Ride it.

It will be such a horror to remain.

THE GODS REMEMBERED ME

The gods have been good to me.

They have given me
what most kill for.

Not the fame.
Not the money.
Not the women.
Not the things that will
leave the people swimming
in flames.

The gods have been good to me.

They gave me art,
it screams from my bones.

They gave me juice,
style, flavor, and it pours
from my skull and heart.

I tilt my heart and knives fall
from its corners.

These people do not understand ...

to wake up and keep your sanity,
what is left of it.

The gods have been too good to me,

and nothing else is needed
other than that.

THE GLOOM IN THE EYES

I am not here anymore.

I have no connection
to the walls
inside this room,
to the gloom that enters
through the window,
and the gentle music
that sneaks out
of the radio.

If you are gone,
then I, too, am gone.

And it makes me feel
like I am drifting
into the ocean,
like a small child
seduced by the sea.

FIGHT THE SYSTEM

So you want to fight against the system?

Stop buying their products.
Stop buying the things they sell us,
the things we do not need.
Stop giving in to their hype,
their distraction.
They want you to think you need it,
with their clever ways they make us all
think we need it.

MKUltra is in the advertising.

No one is safe, not even the children.
They grow with altered brains
and manufactured thoughts.

Fight. Fight. Fight.

Stop giving them power.
They have become gods.
Gods without faces
and gods with no native feeling.

Gods that carry a half truth
and roll it toward the sky.

It thunders. It clouds.

Stop buying their fucking products.

Their domination will fall
quicker than Google can search
how they fell.

ENOUGH ROOM OUT THERE

I had to go.

There wasn't enough
for me here.
I got that feeling long ago.
I knew I had to go
but I overpassed my welcome
long enough.

"Go ahead and leave.
You will be back anyway," she said.

She was always right,
and I hated that.

"And I would understand
if you came back different.

There is a lot to lose
and find out there,
more than you'll ever know."

I couldn't reply,
there weren't enough words.

Maybe that's what I was looking
for, some kind of revelation,
and I knew I wasn't going to find it here.

The answers weren't
going to fall from the sky.
I knew I had to get up
and find salvation
on my own.

LET TO LIVE

And so I am left to live.
I am left to go on by myself.
The trees have abandoned me.
The air in my lungs,
and the clouds on the sky
have moved away from me.

All is too quiet.
All is naked and cold.

The poems have gone
out of mind, out of heart,
to jump into the depths
of the fire.

Have I become less?
Have I gone to the point of no return?

More things wrong than good
and more wrong things happen
to good people than bad.
The world is so fucked up
but I, too, am fucked up.

There is no right in this.
If the mother is mad then
the child is mad
and together we walk away.
Together we are meant
to go on alone.

Sometimes that is the only
thing we share.

AND STILL AND STILL

Things become old,
things become lost,
and sometimes
things become still.

We are becoming
and the days are beginning
to lose themselves
within themselves,

and all is still.

We are still,
and terrible it is,
how all we can do is watch,
as the things

we wish to love
pass us by.

ALL IS WELL AND ALL IS GOOD

I am here now.
Alive and well,
but ultimately thankful
to be alive at this moment.
Inside my small room.
It feels good to feel
my dog push against me.
It feels good to lay here
with my woman beside me.
The smell of our covers
and the cold air blowing
from the vent.

The television is on mute.
The light flickering gives me
peace.

Their breathing gives me peace,
it eases the pain.
It feels like the ships have sailed
and all is well and all is good,
too good.

Tonight hell has frozen over.
Tonight I am not alone.
It is the little things
that give me life.

The little things that give me meaning,
while everything else
doesn't seem to connect much at all.

This must be what life is all about.

ALWAYS FOR MORE

I need chaos.
I need movement.
I need something to happen.

Something horrible,
like a fatal car crash.
Something magnificent
like a child being born.

Just give me something!
I'll take anything.

A man can lose his mind
without his art.
And a man can lose his
art without something
happening: something
that makes him lose his
goddamn mind.

What a terrible need.
What a terrible monster
to feed.

This mind.
This heart.

Always needing to come out.
Always demanding
to be more.

THE MIDDLE OF NOWHERE

In the middle of nowhere
you will find the perfect place
to grab a coffee.

In the middle of nowhere
you will fall in love with a stranger.

In the middle of nowhere
something will happen that
will bring laughter to you for a lifetime.

In the middle of nowhere
you will make a life-changing decision.

In the middle of nowhere
you will stay up all night
and think about what just happened.

In the middle of nowhere
you will find yourself.

In the middle of nowhere
there is a somewhere.

In the middle of nowhere
you will stay a while.

Something different
will happen soon.

Your moment is right
around the corner...

in the middle of nowhere.

THE THINGS WE DO NOT SAY

I will tell you to
get up in the morning
and face the world.

I will tell you to be strong
and fight, keep going.
I will tell you everything
will be okay.

I will push you, inspire
you, motivate you, and
encourage you to be more.

I will not stop.
I will continue.

You are so much more.
You can be anything,
all you have to do is believe.

But it is a shame,
how we know what is good
for others,
but don't know what is good
for ourselves.

Listen to yourself,
and listen often.

Doing so will be
the kind of thing that will
save you.

Save you from killing yourself
or killing someone.

Listen to yourself.

You know yourself better.

Don't let the voice inside
of you get away.

A HAPPY LIFE

To live a happy life:
it is simple.

All you have to do
is try not to get yourself
killed or thrown in jail.
Stay away from anything that
threatens the life out of you.

Meet good people.
Meet bad people.
Love good people.
Love bad people.
Leave good people
Leave bad people.

Do everything in twos:
both good and bad,
live both on the edge
and then, forget everything
and go again, begin again.
You will live the same
life at least 10 times.
You will see it all for what
it is: good or bad.
You will know this,
and you will still not learn
how to get away from it.

It is all around you:
good and bad.

Just remember...
try not to get yourself killed.

A PHONE CALL

Banging away at the old typewriter,
it has been a long night.
I had a deadline with my art agent.

"Listen up there rmdrk,
I need five pieces from you,
and I need them all done by Friday."

Hell, it was Tuesday.

"Yeah, I will get those done for you on time."

I went to the art store, goddamn, it was expensive.
I spent 680 dollars on 5 canvases
and about 150 dollars on paint,
and a few extra brushes.

You would think after spending almost a thousand
dollars that they would have at least thrown in
the brushes.

I bought 5 of them.

I didn't sleep for nearly 70 hours.
My body was exhausted and I was working
on the floor, I just wanted to die!

The whole time I wished I had more time.

By the time Thursday night arrived, I gave
my agent a ring.

"I got all the work ready."

"That's great to hear, but all the canvases
are not due till next week, but thank you for
getting them done."

He hung up the phone.

All that fuss and trouble to hear that.

A phone call could have saved me from thinking
about suicide.

Sometimes communication can save a life
and sometimes that is all it takes.

THE HUNGER OF THE ART

There are too many things I want to say
and not many words to use.

To this I live tonight.

For all the people who make art
without knowing how to do so.

If the god gene is inside of you,
let it run out of you.

To create is a terrible sickness.
One no one ever seems to get away from.

Artists die with questions on their hands
and not enough answers in the world
to complete them.

This hunger will never cease to exist.

It goes on and on and on.

And on.

I HAD A DREAM I WAS HUMAN

I had a dream I was human
and it was a nightmare.

Crowds upon crowds.
Walking slanted, bumping into each other,
mindless.

There was no moral.
There was no justice.
There was nothing to remember.

Countries welcomed by the fire and the arms.
Countries burning countries.
Countries becoming less like countries
and more like prisons.

I had a dream I was human
and it was a nightmare.

Buildings on top of buildings.
Some would fall and some would rise,
but none would keep still.

There were knives on people's backs
and the pain that followed never lost its breath.

I had a dream I was human
and it was a nightmare.

Alarms go off as guns go off
and the people jump off:
out of their goddamn minds,
out of their goddamn bodies
and more.

Into small apartments that feel like cages
and into restrictions that look like laws.

Their freedom was manufactured.
Their democracy was neo-communism.
Brands forced slavery and the banks
controlled it all.

I had a dream I was human
and it was a nightmare.

A terrible nightmare.

Somebody please wake me up.

Somebody please get me the fuck out of here.

POETRY IN THE BLOOD

I sit here watching as the world
comes to an end.

Pouring more drinks with my comrades.
Pouring more soul into the earth:
the ground holds a blood we no longer have.

All the people still do not love one another,
they flourish in the pain till their last day:
it is all they know how to do.

No one knows why we are like this
and no one ever will.

We are all the things they warned us about,
seduced by celebrity, starved by destruction,
controlled by the money
we are not meant to see.

The world is burning
and we, too, are burning
and we will continue to burn,
until our ashes rise

and

what is left behind
becomes the poetry

we will never live to read.

SEE HER GOING CRAZY

I can see her going insane,
walking past the people,
walking toward the wine,
and the poetry and the music.

I can see the fools surrounding her.
Dying for her attention.
Dying to sleep into her,
to wake up the next day half alive.

I stand before her across the tables,
and the bar and the speakers.

She catches my eye with her eye
and it drifts into the vibration of the night.

She smiles and I laugh.

I do not care enough to do something about it,
but I am like that most of the time.
And I think most people are like this
most of the time too.

No one wants to walk across the room
for a pretty face.

That kind of beauty doesn't last.

Sometimes it takes more to get you going.

But yeah, I can see her going insane,
inside, and out of her pretty face.

IN ALMOST ALL WAYS

In almost all ways,
whether I went to a bar
or a coffee shop
or any type of social endeavor,
everyone always looked happy
or so it seemed.
Everyone had nothing to do
with me, and yet,
in almost all ways,
I felt consumed by it all.

I knew I was out of my senses.
I was closer.
I was out of control.
I was connected
and that was the curse:

I was here but I wasn't.
I knew people but I felt like a stranger.
I left but I wasn't gone.

In almost all ways,
I could not recognize myself,
unless,
I recognized the world
for what it was.

ALONE ALONE ALONE

I am alone,
but I am with someone
and she, too, feels alone.

We drink and laugh and sleep
and party and work
and work and work alone.

God created the universe alone.
Walt envisioned Disney World alone.
Rowling wrote Harry's story alone.
Phelps won medals alone.
And Steve Jobs died surrounded by his family,
but ultimately he died alone.

We live and we die alone,
but tonight I am with a woman
and she, too, sees the world
the same way I see the world.

And that makes me feel like we are together.

I understand her and she understands me
and maybe we all understand each other,
but even so,
that is something we have to figure
out alone.

THE GIRL ON THE TRAIN

This woman I met.

I thought everyone was like me.
I thought we were all waiting to die,
alone or not,
but ultimately
waiting to die.
I thought life was full of distractions,
things we have been told.

You go to school.
You make friends.
You get a job.
You get married.
You buy a house.
You have a child.

A child will make things better.

I thought everyone was insane to live
by these rules.
Then came this girl,
with a smile that would burn
the hell out of you.
A thousand suns in her eyes.
She wasn't like me or like anyone
I had ever met.
This girl was really happy.
She stayed up late.
She ate breakfast after noon.
She quit her job because it was full of shit.

She was mad.

She was a wild beast,
a free bird on fire.

The world called her crazy,
but I thought she was one of the gods.

She did what she wanted,
and that was a rare thing.

She knew something,
something the rest of the world
wasn't ready for.

She knew how to live
and she would smile like she knew
this secret, stare at us
and lightly laugh.

And all of this, while we watched her
in our little rooms
waiting to die.

The world is not ready to be free.

LIVING MACHINES

Do not miss me when I am gone.
If I have to go then I have to go.
The same way you would leave
if you had to as well
and you would tell me not
to miss you.

But before I go I want you to know one thing.

Learn how to see the best
and the worst in people.
Learn how to separate the two.
Learn how to see through faces and smiles.

Most are beautiful but beneath it all,
most have a terrible need to
devour people for their own interest.

Do not give yourself away.

Make yourself valuable, my dear.

You are rare and everything you have to offer
should be paid in blood
and sweat and tears and love
before you are gone.

Before you arrive in the next life.

The next place where I will find you
and we will rest there for the last time.

THEY DO NOT WANT YOU TO KNOW

Here are some things
they don't want you to know.

They process the food.
They jack them up with chemicals
because it helps the food last longer
and it is cheaper to mass produce.

Here are some things
they don't want you to know.

You get sick from eating these foods
and you are forced to see a doctor:
this is why Americans are forced to have
health insurance.

Here are some things
they don't want you to know.

You are prescribed medications you don't need,
some even worsen the human body.

Here are some things
they don't want you to know.

AIDS, Ebola, the flu and other viruses
were created in a lab.

Here are some things
they don't want you to know.

JFK was the last real president.

Here are some things
they don't want you to know.

The oxygen isn't pure anymore.
It is filled with too many substances
and it is killing us slowly.

Here are some things
they don't want you to know.

The illuminati is real.

Here are some things
they don't want you to know.

You are programmed to believe
all the above is a conspiracy.

Look at the world around you.

If you look at your phone every 15 minutes
to look at the same thing you just
looked at 15 minutes before — they got you.

Wake up,

the American dream is a nightmare.

CLOSER TO OBJECTS

I am not sure about everyone else

but the moments I do not hear from anyone
are the best of moments.

And in these moments I feel alone
but I also feel at peace.

In a strange way,
not having anyone
around makes me feel
as if I am the last human on earth.

It makes me appreciate everything.

It takes me closer to it all.

To Charise:

May your flame live
within me,
and continue to
inspire me
through every
waking hour.

With open eyes I see the world,
with an open heart I see the souls,
and with an open mind I see it all differently.

Thank you for your time.

Robert M. Drake

CHASING THE GLOOM

COMING SOON

SUNFLOWER

ROBERT M. DRAKE

A NOVELLA
COMING SOON...

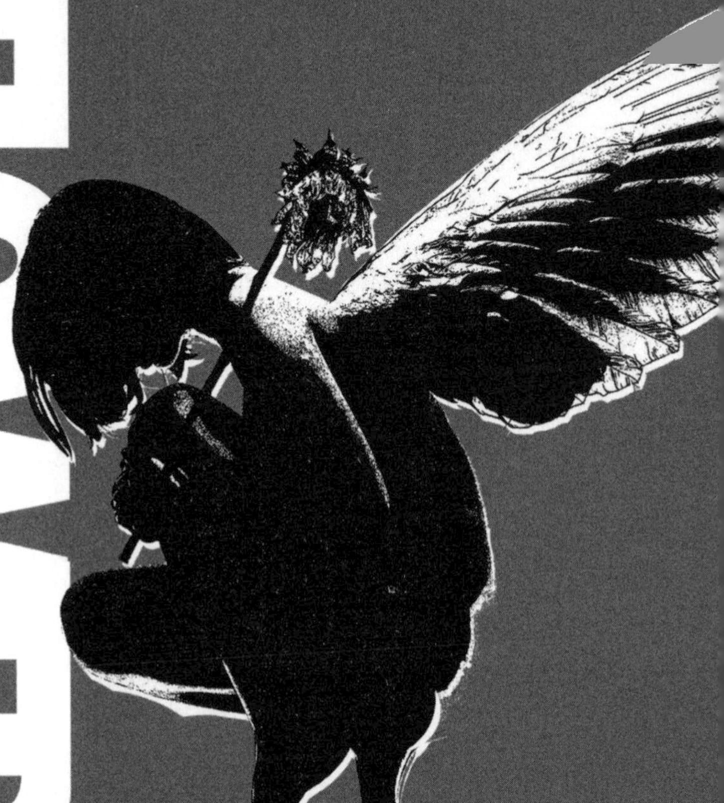

Also Available
ROBERT M. DRAKE
SPACESHIP

Also Available

ROBERT M. DRAKE
SCIENCE

ROBERT. M. DRAKE

beautiful
CHAOS

Follow R. M. Drake
for excerpts and updates.

Facebook.com/rmdrk
Twitter.com/rmdrk
Instagram.com/rmdrk
rmdrk.tumblr.com

To Gui,

You keep living my brother.

You will never die.

Maybe one day I will find you
and we will laugh
and I will see you
for the very first time.

Rest in paradise my brother.